SOUL REBELS

THE RASTAFARI

WILLIAM F LEWIS

late of John Jay College of Criminal Justice,
City University of New York

with Foreword by
Serena Nanda

Edited by
Joan Young Gregg

WAVELAND

PRESS, INC.

Prospect Heights, Illinois

For information about this book, write or call:

Waveland Press, Inc.
P.O. Box 400
Prospect Heights, Illinois 60070
(708) 634-0081

Cover: Rasta with dreads, eating. (UPI/Bettmann)

Contents

Foreword

Serena Nanda

John Jay College of Criminal Justice, CUNY

Writing this foreword to *Soul Rebels: the Rastafari*, fills me with both joy and sadness. Joy, because of the important contribution this book makes to the ethnographic literature, and sadness because William Lewis' untimely death, in July, 1992, prevented him from seeing its publication.

William Lewis brings a new, original perspective to the study of the Rastafarians, a social movement that began in the 1930s, in Jamaica, West Indies, and continues to find adherents in the United States, England, Ethiopia, and other places around the globe, as well as in Jamaica itself. Because of the Rastas' endorsement of rebellious attitudes toward the authority of the political, economic, and cultural establishment, and particularly because of their use of marijuana, in defiance of state law, the Rastafari have been described as a bizarre subculture, identified as a revolutionary movement, and summarily dismissed as a cult.

Lewis rightly called these reductionist perspectives into question. His work reviews some of these positions, but most importantly, suggests another perspective from which to analyze Rastafari culture. *Soul Rebels* places the ganja-smoking and otherwise defiant participants who make up the Rastafarian community in a struggle against the bourgeois world from which they emerged. Equally important is the emphasis Lewis puts on diversity: the Rasta movement is not monolithic. Lewis' analysis emphasizes this diversity because understanding the varied societies in which Rastas find themselves is critical to understanding the local meanings they embrace. Rastas function in strong capitalist state societies such as the United States, in economically developing states such as Jamaica, and in weak states, such as Ethiopia. Hence, the study of the historical development of the Rastafari implies a reflection on state society. In addition, the Rastafari take on different appearances in urban and rural contexts. This setting of local ethnography in a wider political context is another major contribution of Lewis' work because the relationship between the local community and the state in which it is situated has important implications for the ways in which Rastas pursue their meaningful lives.

To support Lewis' unique perspective, *Soul Rebels* presents ethnographic materials, not often included in texts on the Rastafari, which have their source in his fieldwork in a fishing village in Jamaica, a commune in Ethiopia, and smoke shops in a large city in the United States. It uses these ethnographic data to examine the Rastafari culture in its confrontations with the law, its growing ambivalence about itself, and the continued resistance of many of its adherents to the dominant bourgeois culture. In this approach, Lewis' work owes much in its theoretical foundations to the work of Victor Turner and to radical social theory, both of which are needed to avoid the reduction of Rastafari to a political or economic movement or a millennial cult.

Soul Rebels grows out of William Lewis' long standing anthropological interests in religion and social movements, as well as a personal commitment to Roman Catholic liberation theology. For those of us who knew Bill, it is no surprise that he chose to work with the Rastas, as he was a bit of a soul rebel, even a trickster, himself. It is also no surprise that Bill would go beyond any reductionist theory in his analysis. In his own multiple identities as Catholic priest, Franciscan brother, research anthropologist, teacher, counselor, and interdisciplinary scholar with degrees in anthropology, theology, philosophy and music, Bill defied any simple categorization. Like Victor Turner's liminal figures, Bill bridged many structures and brought to his teaching and his research the spirit of *communitas* and cultural critique. As a student of Stanley Diamond at the New School for Social Research, Bill's work reflected both radical theoretical and humanistic concerns. He was committed to bringing the perspectives of cultural anthropology to his own church community through publication and lectures, and equally committed to an anthropology that joined deep concerns with cultural meaning to an advocacy for social and economic justice. William Lewis was beloved by his colleagues and his students for his wit, his intellect, his sensitivity and his commitment. We will all miss him very much.

Preface

The Rastafarian* movement began on the Caribbean Island of Jamaica in the early 1930s. Then as now, the freedom with which the Rastas express individuality and sensuousness moves beyond cultural constraints. Their hair flowing in locks, their dress adorned with the African colors of red, green and gold, their prodigious use of marijuana, and their divinization of Haile Selassie are out of place in a world of bourgeois sensibilities. Rastafari imagery suggests the odyssey of an individual causing mischief amidst the cultural norms of health, religion and civility of the dominant society. At the same time, however, the Rastafarian movement has modified the spontaneity and liminality of its earlier days. Thus, diversity informs my ethnographic materials that extend from the start of the movement until the present.

My conversations with Rastas occurred over a period of five years of intermittent fieldwork. Our exchanges took place in a fishing village in southern Jamaica, an urban neighborhood in the northeastern United States, and the Ethiopian market town of Shashemene. Among those who shared the meaning of their commitment to Rastafari with me were a fisherman, a recluse, a street hustler, a middle-class Jamaican, a criminal suspect and a repatriated Rasta. Our interactions were of a spontaneous nature rather than formalized interviews. Some Rastas I spoke with were reluctant participants in our rationalized and bureaucratized society, while others continued to defy it, rejecting any compromise with Babylon, as they call modern society. The differences I encountered motivated me to recast some social theories on the movement and propose others.

The voices of the Rasta brothers and sisters have allowed me to identify some complexities in the movement. My experience of Jamaican social life, the hegemony of capitalism, and my identity

*I use "Rastafarian" as an adjective, "Rastafar" as noun and adjective, "Rasta" as noun and adjective. This usage reflects the somewhat capricious employment of terms in the literature.

as a white Roman Catholic priest have found their way, too, into this recounting of conversations with Rastas and an analysis of the movement. This self-awareness, rather than being a burden, provides the context for an inter-subjective exchange with the Rastas. The importance of an oral tradition in the religious culture of the Rastafari is not foreign in some circles of Roman Catholicism, especially among those, like myself, who profess a theology of liberation. I believe that the Rastafari have revitalized a folk culture from which they have derived a theology of liberation. The ethnographic description of the Rastas recorded here, then, is a product of my own sharing in their lives, as ambivalent as that was. It grows out of my long held personal and anthropological interests in religion, social movements, Marxist theory, reflexive anthropology and Roman Catholic liberation theology.

Chapter 1, "History of the Rastafari," briefly considers the origins of the Rastafarian movement and its development from the 1930s to the 1980s. The Rastafari developed a unique identity by rallying around Emperor Haile Ras Tafari Selassie I of Ethiopia as their King of Kings and Lord of Lords. In this chapter I identify some of the currents that brought about changes in the movement and Jamaicans' perceptions of it. The economic situation, the changing political scene, and an attempted institutionalization of their charismatic origins by some Rastas are the issues that help us understand the fiery passion behind the origins of the Rastas.

Chapter 2, "A Fishing Community in Jamaica," covers ethnographic materials from a Rastafarian community living on a beachfront in southern Jamaica. Their work patterns, sessions with ganja (marijuana) and rejection of modernity are witness to the resilience and persistence of the movement.

Chapter 3, "Urban Rastas in Kingston, Jamaica," is dominated by the personalities of Nigel, Lion and David, whose conversations reveal the ebb and flow of meanings that Rastas can create under the influence of ganja. Spontaneity and ritual mark their creation and grasp of meanings, as they engage in a dialogue about life.

Chapter 4, "Rastas in a Kingston Suburb," centers around Pierport, a pseudonym for a typical middle-class community in Jamaica. Respectability, sexual roles and Christianity are focused on two Rastas, Lloyd and Gordon, who have accommodated the dramatic qualities of the Rastafarian ethos to fit the context of Pierport, where noneconomic values play a significant role in the lives of its residents.

Chapter 5, "Commentary," is a reflection on the ethnographic material presented in the previous chapters. The spontaneity and freedom that some Rastas express are viewed as patterns of behavior that contrast with the respectability of the Jamaican bourgeoisie. The hegemony of the modern state of Jamaica figures prominently in this divergence of Rastafarian lifestyles from the majority population.

Chapter 6, "The Rastafari and the Jamaican State," continues the discussion of the cultural significance of the movement in a nation which is not yet fully developed in an economic and technological sense. This chapter explores the contrast between Jamaican society, which has not yet arrived at a consensus of interest and a sense of the common good, and the United States, which does possess that sense of a commonwealth. More advanced capitalist societies, such as the United States, can trivialize the meanings of Rastafari through a commodity mentality, but in Jamaica one encounters ambiguous and pluralistic cultural meanings.

Chapter 7, "The Deputy Inspector and the Rastas," narrates an interview with an official of the Jamaican police department. It exemplifies how the Jamaican working and middle class use cultural rather than so-called objective perspectives to understand the Rastas.

Chapter 8, "Urban Rastas., U.S.A.," focuses on a Rastafarian enclave in an urban neighborhood in the United States. Ras, Rashi and Baba II provide us with profiles that express the dynamics of the social drama they enact in their neighborhoods, especially with regard to the law and the police. Implicit here is the question: Are these Rasta criminals, deviants, or religious mystics?

Chapter 9, "Rastas and Symbolic Action," examines the concept of social drama. It attempts to demonstrate that even in breaking the law, Rastas cannot merely be viewed as organized criminals, for whom rational calculation looms large. Rather, they are enacting a social drama in which metaphysics, images and the nonrational figure prominently. What undergirds this discussion is the local context in which Rastas stage their conflicts with the guardians of law and order. When higher echelons of authority inject themselves into the fray, the conflict is no longer played out as social drama, but resolves itself rationally according to the universalist standards of the American legal system.

Chapter 10, "Repatriation," discusses my visit to Shashemene, Ethiopia, and the ambivalence about the meaning of the movement on African soil.

Chapter 11, "Legal Tensions," identifies the Rastas as an ethnic group, fulfilling the ethnic profile by creating for themselves a separate identity in regard to food, language, and the dynamics of their daily life. A review of some legal notions in the United States and Jamaica draws attention to the way in which a capitalist, commonwealth nation such as the United States, tempers the dynamics of ethnicity through its marketplace and legal processes, ensuring that the values of ethnic groups do not threaten the mental and material basis of the market economy.

Chapter 12, "Rastafari as a Social Movement," recapitulates some of the central themes that are woven throughout the text. Will the Rastafarian movement become a platform from which people, especially those of the African diaspora, can launch a rational program for economic gain and civil rights? Or will it recapture its spontaneous elan that cared little for economic adventurism or the political transformation of society into the modern state?

Acknowledgments

When William Lewis died, *Soul Rebels* was almost, but not quite completed; it required reorganization and editing, as well as the completion of many details of production, before it could be published. I had read the manuscript in one of its earlier forms, and shared the enthusiasm of Tom Curtin, anthropology editor at Waveland Press, and the pre-publication reviewers, that it be published. Soon after Bill's death, I suggested to Tom Curtin that we find an editor to put the manuscript into final form for publication, as this would not only be a worthy memorial to Bill, but also make an important contribution to our field. I am very grateful to Tom Curtin for the support that he and Waveland Press have given to the publication of this manuscript under difficult circumstances. I am also grateful to Joan Young Gregg, a highly competent editor, who reorganized her own busy schedule to help complete this work in a timely way. Her own familiarity with the ethnographic literature, as well as her personal friendship with Bill, have resulted in a manuscript very much like that Bill would have completed himself. In addition, I would like to acknowledge the help of Franciscan Brothers James T. Gardiner, S.A., Denis Sennett, S.A. and Wilfred Tyrrell, S.A. and Attorney Thomas Pietrantonio, who were most cooperative in giving permissions and accessibility to Bill's files necessary for the publication of the manuscript. In the Fall of 1990, Bill participated in the Mellon Seminar, "Making Prophecy: Waiting for the Apocalypse," and he often talked about how valuable that experience was for him; I would like to thank the foundation on his behalf for their generous support of his participation. And finally, I know that Bill would want to thank the many Rastas, especially George Batista, who shared their lives and thoughts with him.

1

History of the Rastafari

The Setting

The year was 1930. The pages of the Jamaican press were stirring up the imagination of the downtrodden black population of this island colony with its reports and photographs marking the elevation of a black man, Ras Tafari, to the Ethiopian throne in Addis Ababa. The new emperor was crowned as Haile Selassie I, an Amharic name meaning the power of the Trinity. His scriptural lineage gave him the titles of Lord of Lords, King of Kings and Conquering Lion of the Tribes of Judah. In addition to this biblical imagery, what truly awed the masses of black Jamaicans was that among the retinue of dignitaries paying Selassie homage was the British Duke of Gloucester. That a member of the English royal family should so honor a black monarch of an African kingdom was indeed extraordinary. The splendor of the coronation ceremonies rekindled a passion for Africa in the psyches of many Jamaican blacks whose cultural identity had been eroding under the class and racial segmentation that was taking place on the island.

The year 1930 in Jamaica, as in many nations of the world experiencing the Great Depression, was, economically, a time of misery and unrest among large segments of the population. Until the 1920s, Jamaica's economy had been primarily based on small-scale agriculture, a system considered unproductive and backward by the island's government and business elite. By 1930, capitalism had penetrated the island sufficiently to weaken its agricultural base, and much of the black Jamaican peasantry had been incorporated as wage laborers in the fledgling factories and industries of the

1

cities. The result was social and economic instability which, together with the emergence of various Black Nationalist movements, provided the backdrop against which Rastafari beliefs and culture developed.

The disenfranchised black Jamaican, whether a dispossessed peasant or underemployed factory worker, proved to be a receptive audience for such fundamental Rasta themes as their communitarian economic philosophy and their emphasis on the positive identity of blackness and Africa. The Rastas' adoption of symbolic clothing, hairstyles, and linguistic usages to demonstrate their rejection of middle-class social conventions and wage labor also proved attractive to many. The most visible sign of Rasta identity, their "dreads," or long, uncombed locks of hair, specifically interfered with their participation in wage labor. One Rasta suggested this by speaking contemptuously of those brethren who were tempted to "abandon their faith and culture by running to the barber, so they can go searching within the society of slave drivers for a factory job or a messenger boy job or settle for the worse things in life." The smoking of an illegal substance, marijuana, or ganga, at the Rasta reasoning, or discussion, sessions which form the core of their religious practice, was another aspect of Rastafari culture which allowed the disenfranchised Jamaican to express his opposition to an oppressive capitalist and bourgeois system.

Thus, within a few years of the news of Haile Selassie's coronation, when Jamaican activists such as Leonard Howell, Robert Hinds, Joseph Hibbert and Archibald Dunkley began preaching the message of Ras Tafari (*Ras* meaning Duke, *Tafari* being the Selassie family name), many were ready to listen. The introduction of Rastafari beliefs to the poverty-stricken blacks of Kingston, Port Antonia and the district of St. Andrew proved to be a revitalizing force that eventually spread to other areas of the Caribbean, into parts of the African nations of Kenya and Ethiopia and into urban centers of the United States, England, Canada, Australia and New Zealand.

The message of Howell, Hinds and the others to the Jamaican poor began with a startling revelation: they declared that Haile Selassie was the messiah who was the hope of freedom for all black people. Their voices clashed with those of Jamaica's brown and white elite, who had been encouraging the masses to work productively within the colonial and capitalist economy in American and British companies. In contrast to the work-ethic ideology of the emerging Jamaican bourgeoisie, Leonard Howell proclaimed:

Haile Selassie, Ras (Duke) Tafari, crowned emperor of Ethiopia in 1930.
(Courtesy Department Library Services, American Museum of National History, Neg. No. ZA11265)

> People, you are poor but you are rich, because God planted mines of diamonds and gold for you in Africa, your homeland. Our King has come to redeem you home to your motherland, Africa. The British government is only protecting you until the King comes; and, when he comes, the crowned head of England will turn you over to the King. Ras Tafari is the returned messiah.

A group rallied around this early prophecy that created a novel perspective on wealth, hygiene and politics. Allied to the unique Rastafarian interpretation of their African identity was their rejection of the modernity that was transforming Jamaica in the 1930s. The early Rastas spurned the labor unions, political parties and economic investment that were the basis of the hope offered to the Jamaican masses by the agents of colonialism and capitalism. They rejected the British culture of respectability and even the progress and prosperity that this middle-class ideology seemed to promise the Jamaican worker. Using the imperial image of Selassie as the symbol of their alternate cultural movement, the Rastafarians developed an intensified peasant life dominated by economic communalism, Ethiopianism and a desire to repatriate to Africa. Through their symbolic world, they clung resolutely to the Africanized culture which the peasantry had created, but which had begun to decrease in the 1930s.

The forces that had transformed an independent Jamaican peasantry into a working proletariat receptive to the message of the Rasta movement were set in motion at the turn of the nineteenth century. At that time the American United Fruit Company, with its capital investment in banana production and exportation and its basis in private ownership and profit, was destroying a peasant economy that had previously relied on reciprocity and redistribution. Seduced by the promises of the capitalists, many peasants seized the apparent opportunity to increase their wealth by selling their lands and turning to wage labor.

However, racial stratification, as a means to profit, was evident from the beginning. The mulatto peasants generally profited from the banana trade, accumulated wealth and became the strength of the middle class. Their ascent to economic power was, however, at the expense of the black peasants, who eventually lost their jobs in the economic competition that marked the 1920s and the world depression of the 1930s. Without land or wages, these peasants rapidly depleted their meager savings and soon found themselves penniless.

The Rastas were not the first to respond to the increasing misery of the Jamaican blacks with a message emphasizing African identity and black self-worth. During the 1920s, Marcus Garvey founded his Universal Negro Improvement Association (UNIA) with "negro capitalism" as its linchpin. Garvey wrote:

> Wealth is strength, wealth is power, wealth is influence, wealth is justice, is liberty, is real human rights. The system of our world politics suggests such and as a fact it is . . . It is the accumulated wealth of the Negro that will force him to the front and compel men and nations to think of him in terms of economic justice. All this is achievable through a greater economic expansion.

Garvey's program, unfortunately, unwittingly imitated the interests of a black bourgeoisie, praising the capitalist values of individualism, competitiveness and opportunism. Garvey's vision of businesses owned and directed by blacks fell victim to the entrenched racism of the colored and white intellectuals, for whom blackness meant nothing more than powerlessness and an indolent life of the "ne'er-do-well." This colored and white elite judged the black underclass as incapable of sustaining the discipline required for economic success because of their supposed biological differences. How could such persons be legitimated in leadership roles? Indeed, to be a respectable person one had to rid oneself of blackness by proving white blood in the ancestry or resorting to hair straighteners, bleaching creams and the like—popular products that were advertised in the elitist press, the *Daily Gleaner*. Black identity excluded a Jamaican from any effective participation in the dominant economic and political system.

While Garveyism and the Rasta movement both engaged the unconscious, repressed desires of Jamaica's black people, the two groups had very different ends in view. Garveyism looked to the future and economic progress while the Rastas looked to the traditions of an Africanized peasantry. The Rastas never sought to reconcile blackness with modern concepts of economic development, nor did they participate in reformist programs for the humanization of capitalism, such as labor unions or political parties. In the Jamaican labor unrest of 1938, for example, the Rastas played no role in the workers' struggles for union representation and governmental regulation of labor abuses. In addition to rejecting reform measures and "negro capitalism," the Rastas also shunned the work ethic and the Christian concept of charity, which, along with an acceptance of the inferiority of blackness, were ideas espoused by the rising white and mulatto middle classes in Jamaica.

By the mid-1930s, the black Jamaican peasant was living in miserable conditions. Although, ironically, the setbacks of capitalism during the depression offered some opportunity for Jamaicans to return to their native industries and handicrafts (suggesting a revitalization of the peasantry), this interlude was short lived. As the Jamaican dependency on capital increased, the peasantry became segmented into the rich, the middle class and a landless working class. Most of the peasants had abandoned their way of life to wage labor. These landless peasants formed a pool of unemployed workers throughout the 1930s and 1940s. Their misery was described by one writer in the *Daily Gleaner* in 1934:

> Hundreds of thousands of our people are mere squatters on properties off which they may be turned at any time. . . . There

Jamaican peasant boys from the interior. (United Nations)

is no hope for the prosperity of the peasants until they are settled
on lands of their own. . . . There is too much land monopoly in
this agricultural society.

The spread of Rasta philosophy and the rise of Rastafarian
communities occurred within this context.

Rasta Beginnings

Rejecting the future-oriented ideologies of the working classes and
the rising middle classes, the Rastas etched out cultural enclaves
among the displaced peasantry in the streets and lanes of Kingston,
Jamaica's capital city. Their first settlement, popularly called Dung
Hill but renamed Addis Ababa by the Rastas, was known as a community of bearded men. These Rastas described themselves as
"righteous Abyssinians awaiting again the return of Haile Selassie
to the throne," that is, the throne he had lost in the fascist invasion
of Ethiopia in 1935. As street people proclaiming this doctrine, the
Rastas probably amused the middle class. The urban elites snick-
ered at the Rasta cry that the Ethiopian emperor was the King of

Kings, greater than the British monarch, and that Africa was the true homeland for all blacks. Surely, this was just another humorous irrelevancy with which the "happy-go-lucky darkie" kept himself content, they thought. The Rastas' outrageous claims sounded even more ridiculous to them than had the utopian dreams of the now declining Garveyites for black economic prosperity.

Nevertheless, mindful of Jamaica's previous unsettling experiences with religious movements, the authorities began to arrest the most outspoken of the Rasta leaders on charges of sedition and disturbing the public order. The Rastas were spreading beliefs that did not accord with the role the upper classes had assigned to the blacks. The Jamaican elite regarded the Rastas as followers of misguided teachings, and the Kingston magistrates contended that Howell and the other leaders in the movement were

> intending to excite hatred and contempt for his majesty the King and for those responsible for the government of this island, and to create disaffection among the subjects of his majesty and to disturb the public peace and tranquility.

Howell's arrest and conviction, however, did not stifle the enthusiasm of the "misguided" blacks, who by 1936 numbered around three thousand. The Rasta leader Altamount Reid found a receptive audience at Kingston's Liberty Hall when he confidently proclaimed:

> We are looking to Haile Selassie for the spiritual deliverance of the world, not only among coloured races but white as well. We are working towards a closer unity among mankind. The principles of the organization are based on bible prophecies borne out by the coronation of Haile Selassie in 1930 when he was proclaimed King of Kings and Lion of Judah. We claim him to be the messiah.

While the Rasta movement grew, troubles mounted for their communities, especially during the war years of the 1940s. The media had cast suspicion on a Rastafarian commune called the Pinnacle, which had been set up by Howell as an anticipated refuge from which the Rastas would be safe from the Nazis and the European powers who, Howell believed, were ready to take over the island after the war. In response to his urgings, people sold their goods and possessions and flocked to the Pinnacle, where they followed a lifestyle directed by Howell's Rasta precepts.

The Pinnacle was a scandal to its neighbors and in the press. The ritual codes, and the dress and the behavior of its residents were clearly in opposition to the society around them. Their wearing of dread locks, communal sharing of property and return to subsistent agriculture marked their reclamation of a peasant life which other Jamaicans had abandoned. Of more concern, Pinnacle residents were reported to have no respect for the law, to believe that all lands belonged to them, and to be robbing and terrorizing their neighbors. The Jamaican establishment was particularly disturbed by reports that Pinnacle residents had pressured the owners of nearby lands to stop paying their taxes to the government. In mid-1941, the police raided the commune and arrested Howell, who reportedly boasted at his hearing, "I will teach you that you are not to pay taxes. Neither you nor the government own any land here. I am Haile Selassie."

In 1954, the authorities finally disbanded the Pinnacle commune. After their expulsion, the Rastas returned to the ghettos of Kingston and regrouped. Their membership grew as they lived among the Burru people, a term which meant "wicked" in the Yoruba language of West Africa. Most of the Burru were seen as outcasts and even criminals in the eyes of Jamaican society. Soon elements from the Burru culture began to surface in the Rasta movement. From the Burrus' satirical, antisocial and inflammatory folk music (intended to continue the tradition of protest from the days of slavery), the Rastas learned much about both musical form and social satire, which they later incorporated into their own style of music, reggae. They also took on the Burru's reputation of sheltering wrongdoers who had broken the law or returned from imprisonment. Their association with this disreputable segment of Jamaican society led to increasing hostility against them by the establishment and eventually the authorities burned their shacks in Kingston Pen. The bearded brethren vowed that they would not leave their "father's kingdom for another man's land," however, and the Rastas remained in Kingston to harangue the general population on the evils of "Babylon," the name they used for the established state.

During the late 1950s and early 1960s, the alienation between the Rasta community and the general population increased. When Haile Selassie granted five hundred acres of fertile Ethiopian land to those who had helped Ethiopia rid itself of its fascist invaders, the Rastas received this news enthusiastically. A Rasta gathering supporting repatriation to Africa led by Prince Edward Emmanuel in the Back-o-Wall section of Kingston, resulted in a harsh confrontation with the police. A year later, when another Rasta, Claudius Henry, promised thousands of Jamaicans that the tickets he was distributing bearing Selassie's likeness would guarantee their passage to Africa, he was arrested and charged with treason and possession of a cache of weapons.

Such incidents made the Rastas appear irredeemable to the Jamaican middle class. One letter to the *Daily Gleaner* in 1959 outspokenly characterized the bearded men as

> dirty, lazy, violent, ganja smoking good for nothing rascals using religion as a cloak for villainy, having no regard for the law or other people's property, loud mouths and a general nuisance.

Through the 1950s, then, the Rastas played out a kind of existential absurdity in Jamaican society. They defiled the sacred image of the white Jesus as liberator through their own theology of Haile Selassie, and yet they also offended the spiritualist churches, which were the support of Jamaica's poor, by shunning the practice of possession trances. The Rasta call for repatriation to Ethiopia was a rejection of political involvement in their own society. Their refusal to imitate English mannerisms—the undisputed sign of respectability in Jamaican society—showed a disregard for convention. They viewed marijuana—a drug popular among the working poor as a palliative to help them endure their labor in the cane fields—as a tool of illumination to make one aware of the evils in the bourgeois world. These traits marked the Rastas as a challenge and a threat. Defying the direction of their society, they refused to embrace the cultural assumptions of a growing business mentality, rejecting the profit motive which others thought would lead to the prosperity and progress of the society at large.

The open hostility against the Rastas prompted some of them to invite scholars from the University of the West Indies in Kingston to visit them in their communities. A university team was dispatched into the ghetto, and after gathering information in a whirlwind of fieldwork, the scholars concluded that the "Ras Tafari cult is unique, but it is not seditious. Its adherents have and should continue to have freedom to preach it." The report, which was made fully public in the pages of the *Daily Gleaner*, had a positive effect on popular and governmental opinion alike and decreased anxiety about the Rasta community's activities. One suggestion in the scholars' report, that Jamaican authorities visit Ethiopia in order to investigate the feasibility of repatriation, was eventually implemented, and to this day, a group of repatriated Rastas have been living peacefully as peasants in the Ethiopian land.

The more positive view of the Rastas derived from the work of the university scholars continued into the 1960s, gaining strength from the currents of independence and patriotism which were emerging at this time. Increasing respectability for the Rastas came with Jamaica's political independence in 1962 and with a visit to the island from Haile Selassie. By the 1970s, the Rastas' call for the Africanization of Jamaican society was no longer so out of tune with a racially stratified Jamaica. The Rasta brethren, too, had adjusted to the wider society and were working productively in fishing cooperatives, small farming, hawking and peddling, and such crafts as upholstering, shoemaking and woodcarving.

Also, at this time, some Rasta culture had become more formal through the organization of such groups as the Ethiopian Orthodox Church in Jamaica, the Coptic Zion Church, the Ethiopian African Black International Congress and the Twelve Tribes of Israel. The first of these, the Ethiopian Orthodox Church, whose headquarters are in New York City, was the church of Selassie. Its clergy accommodate some of the Rastas' beliefs, and the "Dreads" who attend that church are under the special protection of its *abuna*, or bishop. The Coptic Zion Church, on the other hand, whose headquarters are in Florida, appears to many Rastas as a false expression of Rastafarian philosophy because of its attempt to modify the movement into a capitalist organization. (Incidentally, the Coptics in Florida were involved in litigation—the first, but not the only, court case of its kind—over their sacramental use of marijuana, an argument they lost in the late 1970s in a Florida state court.)

Another effort at institutionalizing Rasta culture led to the organization of a commune at Bull Bay started by Emmanuel and his followers. This is a quietist group that has no political or economic ambitions aside from those that relate to the maintenance of the commune. They lead a quasi-monastic life, adapting the Judaeo-Christian Scriptures to their beliefs in repatriation and black identity. Their rigid rules exclude menstruating women from the company of men and generally separate the sexes. The community discourages private ownership, and all the money gathered from the sale of the brooms and straw mats which they manufacture and then sell in the Kingston area is communally shared. Their industriousness is acknowledged by Jamaicans who see them daily on public transports and in the streets, greeting all they meet with their traditional salutation, "Blessings." While in public view, these Rasta brethren wear turbans to shield their locks from the gaze of the nonbeliever.

From their tabernacle in their "new Zion" the Bull Bay Rastas offer up daily prayers and chants to the accompaniment of drums. Black identity, salvation and repatriation are the themes of their long rituals, during which they borrow freely from the writings of Emmanuel which are printed in their own publication entitled "Black Supremacy in Righteousness of Salvation." Their praying continues throughout the day, and chants such as the following are incessantly repeated.

O Jah, our strength and our redeemer, cause thine Holy Face to shine upon us, thy children, so we shall be saved, O thou most holy God Jah Rastafari.

We the black people are the ones Jesus laid down his temple for and raised it on the third day.

Repatriation international for those to return back under our own vine and fig tree, Black Africa. The truth has come when black people take up their culture of black philosophy.

We the black Ethiopians are the first people of creation, the first peacemakers, the first Gods and Goddesses of the entire universe.

Faith, if it hath not works, is dead being alone. So are all the isms of the white world such as capitalism, imperialism, which have held down the Black Man in captivity, with oppression, sorrow and pain.

For the wages of sin is death and the gift of the black Christ is life everlasting. I, Prince Edward Emmanuel, the Black Christ, am the God of the living, not the dead.

The Twelve Tribes, a group established by Vernon Carrington in the Kingston ghetto of Trench Town in 1969, is the most formal expression of the Rasta movement. Eventually this group settled along New Hope Road, far from the ghettos and close to the estate of the late Bob Marley. This organization does not manifest the same religious rigor as the Ethiopian Congress in its ritual and communal living. Besides adhering to the Rastafarian beliefs in repatriation, the messiahship of Selassie and the ritual use of marijuana, the organization also believes that the human race is divided into twelve scattered tribes—a division that occurred after the exile in Egypt during which the people of Jah (the Rasta name for God, a derivative of Jahweh) were dispersed. Each tribe is named after one of Jacob's sons, and each is associated with a month of the year. The membership has set up small shops at its establishment on New Hope Road. The members enjoy polemical arguments and unhesitatingly challenge any visitor in their midst to recant his or her beliefs and become Rasta. Generally, they attract those Rastas who see in their organized networks of support an opportunity for economic betterment, especially through the business of reggae music. The Twelve Tribes of Israel has branches in Brooklyn, New York, and it is this group that organized the community at Shashemene in Ethiopia. The members of this group view Rastas outside their organization as imposters.

The Twelve Tribes, the Ethiopian African Congress, the Coptic Zion Church and the Ethiopian Orthodox Church, then, are the institutions that directly or indirectly provide a public image for the Rastas. These institutions indicate that some Rastas believe in a certain degree of accommodation to society. Certainly, organizational demands such as keeping records, paying taxes and attending to lawsuits have whittled down the spontaneity evident in the Rastas' earlier phases.

In addition to their connection with reggae, the electoral campaigns of the 1970s, with their political manipulation of Jamaica's African roots, helped popularize the Rastas in Jamaican society. During the Jamaican electoral campaign of 1972, the People's National Party (PNP) sifted through the culture of the Rastafarians in order to find symbols that Michael Manley, its candidate for prime minister, might use in his political speeches. Thus, Manley inveighed against the corrupt rich, menaced them with the Rod of Correction, and declared himself a "sufferah's man"—all themes highly revered by the Rastas. Manley's rhetoric politicized the Rastas as bearers of an African identity worthy of emulation by the public. Through his embrace of Rastafarian symbolism he also aligned his party with the interests of the poor who traditionally identified with the Rastas.

When Manley won his election, he introduced his program of democratic socialism in order to reform the abuses of international capitalism in Jamaica. To further support his efforts, he used Rastafarian music to instruct the people on the meaning of the economic reforms. Although his program failed, Rastafarianism still remained useful to political parties. Later on, in the electoral campaigns of 1980, for example, both the PNP and the Jamaica Labor Party (JLP) used Rastafarian symbols and reggae music, even though the hope of turning Jamaica into a socialist state seemed no longer possible.

Nevertheless, not all Jamaicans accepted a favorable image of the Rastas. Many were insecure about the increasing confrontations between the Rastas and the Jamaican state. Perhaps the memory of Walter Rodney, the Rasta social thinker who radicalized the movement, and his violent death still lingered in many minds. Rodney had been assassinated by agents of the repressive government of Guyana in 1980, partly because he projected Rastafarian beliefs onto the class and racial tensions of Jamaica and the rest of the Caribbean. Added to this revolutionary nuance was the Rastas' participation in the overthrow of the dictatorship of Eric Gairy in Grenada in 1979. Both developments signalled to some Jamaicans that the Rastas were a threat to the dominant economic and political system.

In 1981, when the Rasta Bob Marley, the world-famous reggae

musician, died, the new Jamaican administration of Prime Minister Edward Seaga honored Marley's memory with the pomp of a state funeral. Despite Marley's popularity, many middle-class Jamaicans loathed the government's exaltation of the reggae musician to the status of a national hero. Reggae, a musical form embodying a Rasta aesthetic and steeped in the Third World imagery of the Caribbean, was viewed as incendiary, and Marley's lifestyle, especially his avid use of marijuana, offended many. These negative reactions toward Marley's funeral were the first demonstrations of ambivalence toward the Rastafarians during this period of their political favor. By 1983, hostility had increased, and the upper middle class was again registering its dislike for the Rastas in the *Daily Gleaner*, with assaults similar to the earlier diatribes against them.

By this time, the Rastas' situation had changed significantly from what it had been in the 1930s. By the 1980s, the community of Rastas had become a factionalized movement whose various branches could not readily be identified with each other. Some were following Rodney's efforts to unify the "brethren" under a revolutionary banner and to emulate the militancy of the rebels in Grenada. Others, such as the Elders, who lived in the rural interior, kept the "ancient traditions" alive and avoided political involvement. But although the movement could no longer be identified with its earlier spontaneity, at its essence it remained an assertion of the cultural traits of the Africanized peasantry.

The communalism and cooperative efforts of the early Rasta settlements, such as the Pinnacle and the Zions in Kingston, linked them to the poorer agricultural class and its displaced urban descendants. The Rastas derived their cultural identity from the material and ideological world of the peasants. Fueled by the symbols of Ethiopia and its ruler, Selassie, the Rastas affirmed the peasant's identity with the soil and with extended kin. While the Jamaican capitalists made their work ethic sacred by associating it with their image of a white Jesus, the Rastas used the symbol of the Ethiopian emperor to make the history of the black peasant sacred.

The symbols used by the Rastas were by no means mere romantic fantasy. The blacks in Jamaica had evolved a viable culture from African memories. The peasants throughout Jamaican history had resisted total subservience to outside influences through their community-oriented structures and their open, or "higgler," markets. These emancipatory practices were present even within the constraints of plantation slavery and flourished with the establishment of the free town after the abolition of slavery.

While the whites and mulattos' belief in Jesus may have

legitimated a stratified society in which the blacks were the underclass, the Rastas drew upon their belief in Selassie to elevate the black experience. They shattered the stereotypes that the upper classes had created for the black person as the feckless "quashie," a fictional character devised by the whites, who was unworthy of the community's respect. For the Rastas, the belief in the divinity of the Ethiopian emperor represented more than a religion; he also symbolized their cooperative work effort, their respect for life, their opposition to abortion and birth control, and their allegiance to a large extended family of "Israelites."

The symbol of Selassie as Jah, or God, interfacing with Ethiopianism recast the black experience of the peasantry in imagery that could not easily be copied by the brown or white classes. The trend toward modernization in Jamaica did not daunt the creativity of the peasantry any more than the wretchedness of slavery had. African slaves had preserved their African heritage, not as sterile replicas of the past, but as creative and adaptive local meanings. Thus, the Ethiopian Baptist Church, the United African Church, and so on, were not simply ways that blacks had acculturated themselves to plantation life, but were, in fact, avenues for maintaining an African identity by reformulating African myths, curing rituals and kinship patterns to suit their new environment and local knowledge. Hence, Ethiopianism flowed through the experiences of the peasantry as a body of values, norms and meanings that sustained their African heritage.

Early in their history, the Rastas, in encouraging networks of reciprocity and conceiving their social reality in opposition to the economic and political interests of both the capitalists and the socialists, had set themselves apart from middle-class society much as the peasants had done. In their early ghetto enclaves, called by such suggestive names as New Zion and Abyssinia, the Rastas upheld the traditional values of the Jamaican peasantry and its unique configuration of African traditions dramatizing the peasant way of life.

The roots of the Rastafarian movement are, thus, primarily existential and historical, rather than cultic and millennial, for the true millennialists are those who dream of perfect progress in the future, not, as the Rastas do, in the present. Perhaps the Garveyites and labor unionists were the utopian thinkers and the futuristic dreamers, while the Rastas were the real rebels, conserving and defending traditional values and institutions against those who would change them.

Today's diversity in the Rasta movement has produced a complexity which is overwhelming to the observer. On the one hand, some Rastas still appear in a state of conflict with society. They let their hair grow into long locks in imitation of the lion's mane, sport accoutrements ablaze with the green, gold and red of African patriotism, engage in a prodigious and spectacular use of marijuana, and engage in an underground economy. Wherever they settle, they are likely to arouse the interest of the police, as happened in a northeastern city of the United States, whose police department produced a training film on the dangers of the Rastas as a way of dealing with the "Rasta threat."

On the other hand, some segments of the Rastafarian movement have found an adaptive niche within modern society. Rastas attend colleges, join trade unions and raise families according to the dominant fashion. These Rasta no longer reject the reproduction of capitalist society with the vigor of their forebears. Their belief in Rastafari has settled into the private domain and does not interfere with the individual's ability to participate in the public sector of economics and politics. They seem *not* to be on the side of the "visionaries, the radicals, the seers, and the charismatic prophets," viewed by some as the core of the movement.

Still other Rasta profess their beliefs as might any other religious believer in modern society. Reggae artists, for instance, often proclaim the movement in terms that remind one of organized religion. Ras Tesfa, a popular reggae musician, expresses his beliefs as follows:

> This is the earth we live on; this is not the spiritually grounded place we think it is. This is a negative place. The only time I find spiritual confidence is when I sit by myself and meditate and find that inner peace, and I grasp for that. . . . There's no place on earth that I really feel at home. Only a mad person would want to be attached to this world forever. These things I've learned through Rasta.

Yet, absent from Ras Tesfa's confession is the confidence in Ethiopianism and Selassie; moreover, his allusions to an afterlife are unusual in Rastafarian discourse. His conceptualization of the movement contradicts that of some Jamaican Rastas whom I met in the 1980s, who reject a belief in an afterlife.

To understand this Rasta plurality, some theorists accept its merging with modern society as inevitable and thus put the matter to rest. Others dismiss the sectarianism of the Rastas as a sign of its inauthenticity, a cloak for imperialism. Neither of these views is compelling enough to understand Rastafarian diversity. It is more fruitful to examine the multifaceted aspect of the movement as a response to different cultural contexts. Rastafarian identity emerges from a dynamic interchange between the group and society and does not simply stem from the voluntary nature of group association.

Modern society has exerted pressure for more accommodating tendencies in the movement by encouraging the Rastas to perform as artists, to operate legitimate businesses and to engage in religious discussion. Some Rastas resist these pressures to accommodate: they continue to prefer the informal economy to trade unions, aggression to acquiescence, and a sexual ethic that separates the roles of male and female in ways that are unacceptable to feminists. For such Rastas, the power of the myths of bourgeois culture have weakened, and they no longer believe that social progress will arrive through a blend of modern political, commercial, and scientific interests. With this segment of the Rastas, the movement emerges as an anti-structural response which breaks down the constraints of society. At this point, Rasta individuals discover the bits and pieces necessary to carry out their ritual drama and reconstitute themselves through the symbolic world of repatriation, Selassie and ganja (marijuana). For these Rastas, these are the moments when statuses are temporarily suspended, role hierarchies are obstructed, and people who once knew their place refuse to accept it.

2

A Fishing Community
in Jamaica

Along a sheltered beach on the southern coast of Jamaica, not far from Kingston, lives a community of Rastas. Situated within a tranquil alcove and remote enough from the surveillance of the city's bureaucracies, the Rastas can prosper without interference from outside influences. Tall shrubs shade much of the area on which the Rastas have built their quarters. The local timber is the source for much of their building materials, but store-bought concrete mixes are available for the more ambitious among them. Viewing the complex of structures from the road which winds above the beach, one can imagine an African village lying just ahead because of the peaked, thatched roofs on some of the houses.

Here, Rastas pursue a life free of the many cares and demands that make up the daily rhythms of their neighbors in the nearby towns. They are not indigent. Their fishing expeditions and garden plots make them self-sufficient. Seldom do they depend on the local markets except perhaps for cooking oil and flour. They do not eat meat, but they raise goats whose milk they drink. Occasionally, they sell some of the herd to the neighboring townspeople. On a weekly basis, trucks deliver beer, soda and ice to the community. With these supplies, the Rastas stock their food stands and cater to the tastes of the Jamaicans who frequently visit the beach for leisure.

The Rastas' reasoning about Haile Selassie and repatriation, as well as their incessant smoking of marijuana, flow into the material basis of their subsistent lifestyle. Indeed, the connection between

17

Traditional fisherman, Port Antonio, Jamaica. (United Nations)

their symbolic and material worlds is unmistakable. They do not espouse an other-worldly faith in the pursuit of spiritual realities alienated from a material world, nor do they profess a secular materialism in a quest for goods and services that has no connection to transcendence. In other words, neither the fervor of a religious revitalization movement nor a hankering after the accumulation of wealth constitute the core meanings in their lives.

The origins of this beach community hark back to the bleaker days of Rastafarian history in the 1960s. At that time, after the police had dissolved the Pinnacle commune in 1954, many Rastas had settled in Back-o-Wall, in Kingston. However, the pattern of life that the Rastas developed in Back-o-Wall was shattered in 1966 by the decision of the Jamaica Labour Party to develop the area, razing it to clear the way for a housing project. They wanted Back-o-Wall to be transformed into a working-class community, the backbone of the JLP's successful electoral campaign. In showing favoritism toward its supporters from the working class, the JLP was following the tradition of patronage that prevails in Jamaican politics. Faithful party members expect their share of the rewards should the party win power in the elections.

The dispossessed Rastas from Back-o-Wall were left to their own devices. These Rastas were not members of the working class, nor were they the idle poor. Instead of wage labor, they pursued their livelihood in handicrafts, marijuana trading and general hustling. When their community was summarily destroyed and replaced by the lower-class housing development called Tivoli Garden, they were infuriated. The government's action led many Rastas to the conviction that the state was not truly concerned about the welfare of the black person.

By 1972, matters changed somewhat. In the election victory of Michael Manley and the People's National Party over the JLP came a decline in the protection of capitalistic interests, accompanied by some leanings toward socialism. Prime Minister Manley promised that his party would never repeat those policies of the JLP that favored capitalistic development to the detriment of the poor. Throughout his campaign and tenure as prime minister, Manley set out to fulfill that promise. It was on that journey that he found the tenets of Rastafarianism compatible with his party's socialist goals.

Throughout the 1970s, the Rastas enjoyed a position of honor in Jamaican society that they had never experienced before. Manley not only gloried in the Rastafarian style of clothing, music and cuisine, turning the symbolic world of Rastafari into a template for Jamaican patriotism, but he also extolled the self-sufficiency of the Rastas.

The ability of the Rastas to prosper without the incentives of capitalist values impressed Manley's party. Rasta characteristics in particular merited emulation and became the signpost of a new Jamaican society based on democratic socialism. The party's goal was for Jamaican society to be free of the interests of foreign capital, the source of misery. Not surprisingly, the Manley administration granted tacit approval to those Rastas who pursued squatters' rights on lands that were not owned privately.

The government's enthusiasm for the Rastafarian lifestyle encouraged several Rasta families to carve out their homesteads on the beachfront. Abandoning the sweltering ghettos of West Kingston and the overcrowded fishing village along the Kingston waterfront, some Rastas moved out and forged an identity in an inlet along the sea not far from Kingston.

A Family

Dread (a popular name among Rastas, which refers to "dread locks," the hairstyle worn by the Rastas) is among those Rastas who left Kingston and built a compound on the sandy beachfront for himself and his family. With his wife, Carolyn, and their three children, Josua, Rebecca and Miriam, he lives on land that is owned by the government. Dread is an expert fisherman and Carolyn sells most of his catch at their concession stand on the beachfront.

Four structures dominate their compound: the sleeping quarters, a reception area for guests, a storage shack and the concession stand. The sleeping quarters and private area for the family is a brick and mortar one-story cottage. It is the only solid structure on the compound that seems capable of withstanding a storm. The storage shack houses spare boat parts and the oil for the outboard motor. The reception area is extensive and is shaded by a thatch roof. Here guests can congregate and share a meal with members of Dread's family. The food concession stand hugs the edge of the compound's perimeter and faces outward toward the sea.

Several yards separate the structures from one another. In the yard to the side of the reception area is a corral for the family's goats. Near the sleeping quarters is a fertile garden where ganja and vegetables grow, in addition to some herbs that are used for home remedies. Directly in front of the sleeping quarters is the yard where Carolyn washes the family laundry and Dread works on the repair of his fishing nets. The most secluded yard is the enclosed space behind the guest pavilion. Here the Rastas gather for their reasoning sessions when they visit Dread. The children spend most of their day in a sandy yard at the entrance to the compound, where too, the casual passer-by is welcome to stay and enjoy the cool shade provided by a tall tree, as well as exchange greetings with Dread and perhaps engage him in philosophical conversation.

Furnishings are sparse: a few handmade wooden chairs and a work table. A wood-burning stove and the simplest of utensils are all that is required to put together the family meals. Prepared outdoors, the meals of fish and home-cooked sweet bread are taken when convenient and without much ado. Recently, Dread had installed a power line, but excessive and mysterious overcharges by the utility company caused him to rethink the matter. There is no indoor plumbing, and drinking water is collected from the water pipe that runs through the compound.

Dread is a patriarch. About five feet six inches tall with a lean and muscular physique, he is a masterful fisherman with a keen sense of the tide's moods and tempers. Dread busies himself throughout the day in various ways. He attends to his nets, weaves new fishing lines from bits of cork and a strong twine, and oversees all the business that connects his family to life outside the compound. He supervises the education of the children, deals with an ever-encroaching government agency called the Urban Development Corporation, and pays the bills owed to the firms from which they purchase the foodstuffs for the concession stand.

A distinct regimen of personal hygiene pervades Dread's philosophy about life. Ganja is a source of pleasure to him, and more importantly, he shares a confidence in the healing and guiding effects of ganja with the other male Rastas. While repairing his fishing nets, navigating his outboard or simply lying about the compound, he usually smokes his spliff, a thick wad of marijuana rolled in paper from a brown paper bag. Every Friday, the Sabbath day for many of the Rastas, he retires to the private quarters, where, cut off from everyone else, he fasts and administers purgatives to himself in order to cleanse the interior of his body. His personal concern over cleanliness and use of ganja as a healing herb are traits shared by the other Rastas on the beach.

Carolyn spends most of her day caring for the children, doing the family wash in large aluminum buckets, cleaning the catch of fish and preparing the meals. She also manages to find the time to attend to the needs of customers who order fried fish at the concession stand. She neither smokes ganja, as some women do, nor does she participate directly in the world of the men. She tends to limit and guard her contact with other men: only a handshake, if that, may come between her and another male, and she reserves a chaste kiss for her father and brothers. Whatever free moments she has are spent playing with the children, attending to their needs and occasionally gossiping with visiting female relatives and friends. She seldom leaves the compound, except for a trip to the store to purchase coconut oil or a rare trip to the dentist when the home remedy of ganja and rum fails to bring relief.

Carolyn is a source of honor and esteem for Dread because her virtue is beyond reproach. Both Dread and Carolyn agree that a woman must take a subservient position to a man. Dread once confessed that he finds it necessary to take the whip to her from time to time, because he claims that she gets lazy if not reminded of her duties. Carolyn says that this is their way.

The children, Rebecca, age 11, Miriam, age 8 and Josua, age 4, attend the local basic school, an alternative means of education for the young rural poor. A noncertified teacher conducts the classes in the rudiments of reading and writing, a minimal education that certified teachers find unsatisfactory. As already mentioned, Dread supervises the children's schooling. He only permits them to attend the basic schools because neither he nor Carolyn have the time to teach them reading, writing and math. Dread suspects that the school might turn the children from the ways of the Rastas and inculcate in them the "lazy" ways of reasoning that are prevalent among the non-Rastas. Hence, he constantly inquires about the children's lessons and searches for other basic schools that are more disciplined and demanding of the children. Dread explains that he wants his children to be highly educated in ways that will empower them to resist the "greed, avarice and violence of Babylon." He seeks for them a "roots" education that will respect his culture.

When not at basic school, the children's daily routine is filled with both work and play. Helping their mother clean the fish and haul

Squatters' school, interior of Jamaica. (United Nations)

water and bottles of soda to the food stand are some of the duties that fall upon Rebecca and Miriam. Both are quite talkative with the visitors to the beach who happen to pass by the compound. They are always on the watch for admirers who might fawn over them and from whom they can then expect gifts of candy and other sweets. Dread simply tolerates their behavior.

Josua is the youngest child, on whom great affection is lavished by the whole family. Dread expects Josua to be a skilled adult, a spirited organizer of people and a wise arbitrator for people's rights. He does not believe that Josua should be a fisherman unless that is his choice. As are most of the Rastafarian children, Josua is socialized into a domineering male role. This process begins with an unashamed display of maleness. Unlike his sisters when they were his age, Josua at four is allowed to roam about the compound in various states of undress and enjoys flying through the air on a tree swing with scarcely a stitch of clothing covering his body. Dread justifies the nudity of his son as an expression of the natural-ness of Jah (God). Josua's sisters, however, are never allowed the same freedom to expose their bodies and females in general are not allowed to express the body's naturalness with the familiarity that the male Rastas demonstrate. On the contrary, female sexuality is protected and hidden. While Dread may strut about the compound with pants barely held up by a string at the waist, threatening to come undone at any moment, Carolyn's dress covers her body securely, is never loose and modestly conceals her femaleness.

The entire family is entrepreneurial. When their Jamaican customers visit the beachfront, they can purchase Red Stripe Beer, the local D & G sodas, and Dread's catch of tropical fish. Red snapper, which Carolyn fries in coconut oil along with a sweet bread called "festival," is the favored dish. Sometimes Dread may even hire local townspeople to assist Carolyn on those days when the number of visitors to the beach becomes taxing. This particular beach is popular among Jamaicans because it is a setting where local people can pass a pleasant day free from the stares of tourists, unlike the atmosphere of the beaches on the northern coast.

The prices at Dread's stand are reasonable and geared toward the pocket of the average Jamaican. A bottle of Red Stripe, for instance, costs four Jamaican dollars (about eighty cents in American currency). On the north-coast beaches, which cater to the tourist trade, it might cost ten to fourteen Jamaican dollars. However, foreigners visiting the Rastas' beach must beware. Although there is a generally understood price for food and drink, the Rasta entrepreneur might very well extract a bit more from the white stranger who is not accompanied by a Jamaican companion.

According to Dread, such price manipulation is justified because whites have more, and therefore, they should give more—a common belief among many Rastas. Those accustomed to the democracy of an impersonal cash nexus may be scandalized by the ethic that guides the business affairs of the Rastas: if one has, one gives.

Dread

The family centers on the personality of Dread, who moves through a world of practical affairs, reasoning about the meaning of transcendence and resisting the tides of modernity. I had the opportunity to talk with Dread about his conversion to Rastafarianism.

Dread embraced the Rastafarian philosophy at the age of twenty-two. He came from the interior of Jamaica and was born of peasant stock. His recollections of those days bring back images of how his parents tried desperately to imitate the upper classes. They judged everything according to the norms of the elite, whose beliefs and activities one could read about in the *Daily Gleaner*. Through its pages one learned that clothing, education and manners revealed one's status and respectability, or lack of them. In Dread's opinion, his parents sought after wages and patronage, a world that met the approval of the Baptist ministers.

"I studied the King James Bible and began to see how concrete Jah was. With all of their praying and hand clapping, the Baptists were far from the real God," Dread states. According to Dread, after this realization, his association with the membership of the rural Baptist church then became insufferable.

At twenty-two Dread left the Baptist church and examined the teachings of Rastafarianism. From their encampment near his home, the Rastas' drumming and chanting throughout the night seemed to beckon him. He frequented their gatherings even though his parents feared that he was participating in the worship of the devil. He found it quite the contrary. Their strong male bonding, sense of power, self-assertiveness and celebration of African ancestry transformed him. He particularly recalled how a chant, "Fire, Rasta, fire," and its setting against the beating of the drums stirred him to a new awareness of identity. From then on, he slowly and progressively realized that God was in his flesh, his own body, the incarnate truth. The God in Heaven preached by the Baptists was both a lie and deceit designed to hide the glory of black people from themselves. Moved by the memory of his younger years, Dread exclaims: "O ye black race, be not afraid to take unto thee what is of thy race!"

Dread says his initiation into the truths of Rastafari included long sessions of smoking the herb (ganja) and reasoning with the brethren on the shameful values of the rural Jamaicans. These values had turned them from a life close to the land to one in which they labored for more and more money in order to pursue the trinkets of Babylon. In contrast, the Rastas clung to their land as self-sufficient producers. They taught Dread that people were not poor due to a lack of education, idleness or bad manners, the popular understanding of poverty, but because they had lost their independence on the land, their culture and their heritage.

In the beginning of his conversion, Dread was so enamored of the tenets of the Rastafarian philosophy that he left home, clothed himself in beggar's garb and took to the country lanes preaching about the divine presence in the person of Haile Selassie I. He proclaimed that Ras Tafari was the cornerstone of black identity that the builders of the colonial society rejected and that he was preaching liberation and dignity of all black people. "Discovering Rasta truth always leads the person into a complete change. Blackness and Ethiopia are the finest of creatures, the first that Jah created. As for I, it's a European dynasty that destroys all our humanity."

Dread's life as an itinerant preacher was short lived, however, and he set that lifestyle aside to take up several wives and children with whom he settled in Kingston's Back-o-Wall. There he supported himself and his family through his craftsmanship in sandal making, the selling of marijuana to tourists and business people in Kingston, and vending juice drinks and coconut on the streets of Kingston. All of his entrepreneurialism was part of an informal economy, beyond the regulation of the market, and undertaken with the cooperation of other Rastas. When the JLP razed their Zion at Back-o-Wall, Dread joined other Rastas and fishermen along the Kingston waterfront and lived with them through the 1960s. Under the Manley regime, they migrated to the beachfront, and Dread claimed squatters' rights on the land.

Reasoning

A Rasta reasoning session is a communal undertaking in which one shares beliefs about liberation and justice and relates them to the black experience of slavery, colonialism and racism. A newcomer who reasons with the brethren is challenged, mocked, berated, instructed and finally welcomed as a brother (women are generally not involved in this), if his heart has withstood the test and proven itself to be black.

Reasoning takes place in Dread's compound in an enclosed and shaded yard. The men gather around a wooden table in the middle of the rectangular yard while the women take their places at the periphery. Fathers take their male children with them into the center of the group. When the rhythm of the dialogical exchange leaves an opening, the women may fill it with a Christian hymn. Nevertheless, their participation in the session is minimal, and indulgence in the herb is forbidden. Like many male Rastas, those at the beach, for the most part, believe that women are incapable of interpreting correctly the illuminative qualities that the herb possesses.

The order of the reasoning session is quite spontaneous. The flow of ideas and the topics determine the length of time it will last. On a quiet afternoon in August, I learned how a reasoning session takes on its form. Since the session was to take place at Dread's compound, he took the lead. When the brethren gathered, Dread removed from its wrapping a special pipe called the chalice. He filled it with herb and recited the blessing: "Bestow wisdom, knowledge and understanding. May we live to see the testimony come true when the lion and the lamb lie together. Selassie I shall triumph. Is it right for us to uphold the manifestation of the colonial thing, or should we think on our own?" Having blessed the herb, Dread exclaimed with eyes opened wide, "Jah." The rest responded, "Ras Tafari."

The pipe passed from male to male. Sometimes it was handed over to another with a prayer affirming the power of Jah and at other times it moved through the group very unceremoniously.

The spontaneity of this particular session was prompted by my visit to the compound. By then my presence was a familiar sight on the beach. The Rastas used the session as an opportunity to test my heart for its worthiness. Not surprisingly, the first topic was the established church. The Rastas scrutinized the Church of Rome, the Episcopal church and even the indigenous Jamaican beliefs of *pocomania* (possession by spirits) and *obeah* (witchcraft).

"The Churches teach the people about heaven and hell and not how to live." Dread swears neither by the heavens above nor the hell below because they have not been proven. "Earth is abiding. Man is the center. Survival is for everyone. These are central.

"The churches believe in Christ. This is the part of the Church that is not correct. Christ was in the days of Christ. To this day the house of David continues in Ethiopia. So, let us deal with what is now. Let us not be celestial on this side."

Dread then drew deeply from the chalice. After that he passed it to the person next to him. Fire took it and spoke: "The concept that the churches teach is not Rastafari. Rastafari means to be more positive about what is going on in each other. Ganja is the Rasta's source of knowledge and intelligence, the sacrament." Fire affirmed his Rasta culture as a remnant of the "ancient Israelites, and the Israelites are always the forgotten ones."

After instruction on the shortcomings of the established churches, the Rastas turned the session toward an examination of the structures that were developing within the movement. This trend befuddled them. Dread reflected: "Rastafari is one order. It shouldn't be like the Church that has many divinities. Money has changed the livity (lifestyle) of the Rastafari. The system destroys the politics of Rastafari. Look at the Rasta brethren who make money. They don't speak to the poor Rastas. These upper-class Rastas have forgotten that their roots are here. They have not fulfilled the Rastas' theocratic principle. They do not direct money into the community. They make like they don't know you. I see them here at the beach. Then who do they know?

"In the sixties, the Rastas had a united message. In those days, Rastas were here to change Jamaican society into a life based on justice and love according to Jah. Now we are still a long way to Rastafari. We need to destroy the Church and state and build principles among ourselves. The earth is for the people. Mankind is first. Live with more justice with our brother." I nodded in agreement.

Not all the brethren, however, agreed with Dread. Some pointed to the Twelve Tribes as an example of the Rastas' self-subsistence and independence. To strengthen his viewpoint on the foolishness of Rastas who organize themselves, Dread related the discomfort he experienced when he visited the sprawling establishment of the Twelve Tribes. He was eager to share this experience with his brethren. On arrival he exchanged the customary gift of ganja. However, as the tale unfolded, Dread recalled his displeasure with the reasoning that took place between himself and the younger members of the Twelve Tribes.

When they discovered that Dread was accompanied by myself, a "white priest," they berated him for bringing the pope's spy into their midst. The white priest, the Twelve Tribes believed, acted as the agent of the pope, the devil-man who had designs on their freedom. The taunting, questioning and bellicosity marred Dread's encounter with the Twelve Tribes. His assurances and pleas that I, a priest, was truly interested in Rastafarian philosophy and was even kin to Ras Tafari were of no avail.

After his narrative, Dread shook his head in bewilderment. The Twelve Tribes professed themselves to be the only true Rastas. Yet, this encounter with them amounted to nonsense for Dread. He commented on the incident: "The flesh and the blood is the greatest. The Twelve Tribes are like the incense of the churches that persuade people to think the way of the church, the Roman way that killed Christ."

Dread compares the institutional identity of the Twelve Tribes with that of the established church: Both of them are blind; they freeze the words of the Bible, and this means death. Dread points to his flesh as the seat of the unwritten word, incarnate in the living person. This the Twelve Tribes cannot understand.

The Twelve Tribes and the reggae Rastas at Tuff Gong, the estate of the late Bob Marley, trouble Rastas like Dread. They speculate with money, and this causes consternation among some Rastas. Through their concerts and recordings, they acquire large sums of money, but they do not filter the money into the community. The principle that they violate is basic for the Rastas. Fire puts it this way: "You have money. Go share it with your brethren."

The Rastas on the beach resent those Rastas who they believe have become part of the system that they are supposed to reject. Nevertheless, their criticism of the institution of the Twelve Tribes and other Rastas who are middle class draws them into reflection on their own identity: "Rasta is livity and love. He needs no institutional identification. He is natural. The meanings of Rasta are in the animals, the plants and people most of all. Rastafari is a culture for people, and it is not hostile." The institutionalization of Rastafari projects the image of the European world which "has made up the living for the poor class in Jamaica, especially the black man."

This reasoning session continued through the evening. The group finally fell into repose when the men sensed that they had exhausted the topics. They ended their discussion without any ceremony. The women then brought in plates of fried fish and pitchers of fruit drinks. Having enjoyed the refreshments, all returned to their compounds for the night's rest.

Transcendence

By their deconstruction of the psychosocial basis for identity in Jamaican society, the Rastas approach what has been called a liminal state, that is, a suspension of social status. This marginal state is indeed filled with chaos and peril for the individual, but a Rasta's disengagement from status, role and hierarchy also allows that individual to achieve the sublime. This is unlike the Western approach to transcendence, which often depends on exultation, the detachment of the soul from the body, or the exercise of mind over matter.

The Rastas strip one another of status through a ceremony of ritualized degradation. My first participation in such a "reasoning" session at the beach was threatening and alarming. Rasta upbraiding of my status jostled me from my expectations about a religious experience.

"What good is all the writing and learning in the world that our visitor brother has?" "Nothing, nothing." "It brings no good to us. He makes empty words on the page."

"Why does he support the white world of Babylon and live with the Catholic church?" "The Pope is Satan." "The priests are his representatives." "He will fall with the rest of Babylon in the fire of hell if he doesn't use the information he learns from us properly. We can send fire on his head." "Selassie I is the truth, the life and the way. He contains everything our visitor needs. Jesus is slavery. The Bible says so."

Then I was mocked and ridiculed for my obvious inability to draw deeply from the chalice without choking. Their friendliness which ordinarily greeted me turned into a fierce diatribe against all the values that I held dear. The Rastas brought me low through their sometimes vulgar and offensive gestures and language. I resisted all my urges to fight back and weathered their assault without manifesting any fear or perturbation. I did not enjoy this confrontation, but their use of religious metaphors intrigued me, especially because of their liberating potential. After twenty minutes of this degrading ceremony, the mood of the group reversed itself and became mellow.

"All are brothers, black, white, yellow." "The earth is for all of us, our home." "A man is what he is. Jah Ras Tafari is building each man up in strength."

"No power can conquer Rastas. We will overcome any oppression and destruction of Babylon. Our wisdom breaks the chains of white slavery. Here in Zion we are free of Babylon's evils." "We are not like the churches. These are the people who define God and life from written laws. Here there are no laws. Be and say what you like."

Through their mutual exchange in the reasoning sessions, the Rastas set aside the roles, statuses and sociability of their everyday life. The self is set loose and the ego of ordinary life diminishes. This is not to imply that the group absorbs the person in a type of "brain wash." Rather, a new individual emerges without roots in a structural identity but grounded in a sensuousness that can be called a "high" in other contexts. The Rastas achieve this state of liminality by unleashing from their moorings the patterns of identity held by those persons attached to a world of hierarchies and statuses, such as marriage, priesthood, sexuality, title and so on. Rastas even deconstruct the hierarchical values that control their workaday world. Their practical world of fishing jaunts and small-scale businesses wanes as they enter a liminal state. Through antistructure the Rastas press toward transcendence, but they are not in a state of trance. Their reasoning allows them to celebrate themselves as liberated people, a pleasurable experience denuded of meanings that can in any way be interpreted as oppressive. Within this intellectual and sensuous endeavor, the Rastas ascend to an "I–n–I" awareness, a Rastafarian usage that joins the person (I) with the divinity (I). In this awareness there is a unity of Jah Selassie I and the creature, an experience from which the Rasta derive an inestimable sense of freedom.

Modernity and the Rastas

The Rastas on the beach lead a lifestyle that excludes the competitiveness of class mobility, union activity and political posturing—all marks of the socially mobile Jamaican. They do not espouse a middle-class ethic. Civil service positions, the prized possession of a Jamaican worker, and the courting of political favors, the stepping stone to lucrative employment, are of no concern to the Rastas. Further, as a people who depend very much on their own industry, they manage their affairs through their own sense of justice rather than through a process mediated through the law enforcement agencies of the state. The intervention of the police in their affairs is unthinkable. The Rastas handle the theft of a goat, for instance, by bringing a fierce reprisal against the perpetrator, a type of local justice practiced quite frequently in the rural interior of Jamaica.

Their good health and prosperity belies the fact that the Rastas have no economic plan for the accumulation of funds and for investment in capital expansion. Economic considerations do not inform their use of money, their working day or their enjoyment of leisure time in the same way that capitalism would have it. Instead, they spend their funds on loans, gifts and parties. Thus, their patterns of work, the relationships in the community, the appearance of their dwellings, and their dress remain the same over the years with scarcely a perceptible change. Consumerism is absent among them. There is no commodification of goods and services, and this forestalls any motivation to work in order to acquire and consume more. The Rastas, of course, do set aside some money as a security for emergencies, such as the replacement of an outboard motor or boat. Although these are rather costly items, nothing appears to motivate the group to work any harder or longer than it did the previous day. Fishing trips are undertaken frequently, almost daily, weather permitting, and the nets are in need of constant repair with cork, lead and twine. The women attend to their chores, and food stands when the need arises.

The business of economics does not direct the Rastas, for whom serious discussion, visiting and steady rhythm in daily activity are more important. In the mid-afternoons and evenings, time is spent in conversation, discussion and simply lounging—occasions to share with a fellow Rasta a perspective on the news, the folly of Jamaican society or the injustice that the Urban Development Corporation is planning against the community. While a visitor may find the life of the Rastas tedious and repetitive at best and powerless at worst, the Rastas, when queried about their lack of material wealth and a seemingly precarious existence by the sea, respond by boasting that they have been freed of the drudgery of working for the boss-man.

For the Rasta, differentiation, prestige and hierarchy are not based on the accumulation of wealth, nor on the ability of an individual to amass huge profits. Not one Rasta has a bank account, pays taxes or contributes any information to the census taker. No family is richer or poorer than the others, and resources are freely circulated among the community. Borrowing, for instance, is a popular practice. Accurate records are not kept, and the obligation to return payment is not immediate. Reciprocity is basic in economic affairs among themselves, but this does not necessarily extend beyond the community. For example, marijuana may flow freely among the community as a sign of fellowship, but outsiders must buy it at capriciously determined prices. Overall, then, the Rasta economic system does not generate the invidious class or psychological distinctions of a class-based society. Rather, subordination and superordination are attached to gender, age, marital status and generosity, with the last being perhaps the most significant. The obligation to share is fierce. Rumors around Kingston shortly after the killing of the reggae star Peter Tosh suggested that he met his demise at the hands of brethren to whom he refused a share in his wealth.

The Rastas do not negotiate hierarchy by economic prowess. The power of social mobility or political favor wields no influence on the determination of personal status. The Rastas imagine their relationships as timeless, tradition bound and sacralized by the Scriptures.

For this reason, the community spurns the rich and fashionable reggae Rastas who sometimes visit the beach. They complain that the reggae musicians, popularized since the 1970s through the work of Bob Marley, profit from the Rastafarian philosophy but never share their money with their poorer brothers. The "high and mighty" ways of the reggae musicians irk them, they say, indicating that the Rastas are not impressed by upper middle-class rights concerning private ownership. Nevertheless, they are cordial to their affluent brothers from "Nesta's place [Bob Marley's] up at Hope Road."

The Rastas on the beachfront re-present the drama that has continually confounded the controllers of the state ever since the Rastas' origins in the 1930s. Now as then, the Rastas express little interest in the struggle of the working classes for increased wages and union representation. Indeed, they tend to scorn the debates that the *Daily Gleaner* trumpets incessantly about the necessity for economic development and productivity. Their behavior thus frustrates the intentions of government officials, police officers, and some organized churches who have plans for the economic betterment of Jamaica. The Rastas resist modernization on several counts. They circumvent the centralization required by the capitalist market by engaging in their own entrepreneurial activities, for which they pay no taxes. They reject the values of social mobility and class differentiation through their spontaneous creation of community in the reasoning sessions. They mock the enshrined wisdom of the medical establishment by fostering the use of marijuana. Over all these, the most eloquent testimony of their resistance to modernism is their confrontation with the Urban Development Corporation, which began when the JLP returned to power in 1980 under Prime Minister Edward Seaga. Among its opponents in the beach community, Dread stands out as a leader. He rails against the state's housing projects because they have simply impoverished people.

"Look at them. People sit in those houses. The system gave them hot houses and nothing else. It took away their farmlands and gardens in order to build those houses (pointing across the road to a nearby housing scheme). The houses should sit on the bad soil, not on the rich soil. They should be on the hills, not in the valleys where the soil is rich."

Dread complains that when the system robs people of their land, it leaves them empty, with an illusionary dream about the value of their Jamaican citizenship. This, he claims, is the Babylonian lie and work of the devil.

From the government perspective, the argument for the development of the beachfront on which the Rastas are encamped is clear. For some time, the Urban Development Corporation, under the direction of Prime Minister Seaga, had been trying to dislodge the Rastas and establish a tourist area on the beach. If the Rastas were to vacate the area, tax revenues from the new business in tourism would enhance the state revenues, increase jobs and bolster the economy. As it is now, the interests of the Rastas make that project an impossibility. Nevertheless, capitalization of the beachfront seems inevitable.

Dread and the others do not believe in the argument for progress because their experience tells a different story. "The people of politics protect property and wealth and oppress poor people. If this be democracy in Jamaica, then a new constitution giving equality to all must be imposed on all."

Dread raises a rhetorical question: "What good would it do to transport the Rastas back to the concrete houses or shacks in Kingston? Destruction of our beach doesn't mean progress for us."

Ever since their forced eviction from Back-o-Wall, the Rastas have taken their homestead on the beach as a repatriation. The threats of the Urban Development Corporation do not daunt Dread and the others from refusing to move from the land. Land means justice for the Rastas, and each person should be "under his own vine and fig tree." The beach is their Zion.

The relationship between the corporation and the Rastas is a tense one. According to rumors, the administration pays marauders to steal their fishing traps. From time to time, officials from the corporation drive onto the beach and warn the Rastas that they are interfering with the progress of the people. Still, the Rastas remain. The threat of force has not yet scared them off the beachfront. They will prevail as always, they say, because the beach is their Zion.

3

Urban Rastas in Kingston, Jamaica

Nigel

On a sultry day in downtown Kingston a weary walker might come upon Nigel lounging on his front steps, shirtless, with a towel draped around his shoulders as he carefully dries himself after one of his periodic splash baths. That is how I first met him. A careless observer might take Nigel to be mad, a stigma with which Jamaican society labels the solitary life free from the cares of family and the demands of social responsibility. However, Nigel is affable, courteous and willing to share his wisdom with sympathetic listeners. I was one of them.

Nigel's conversations with passers-by can become serious communications. He interprets such a happy occasion as the result of a mutual consciousness that compels people to reason with him. True communication is never mere serendipity. Once a male stranger (Nigel seldom if ever converses seriously with a female) demonstrates that his interests are compatible with Nigel's, his scrutiny and suspicion change to a more relaxed and intimate tone. Then Nigel asks the visitor to remove his shoes, unburden himself of his baggage, and empty his pockets of money, tobacco, and combs, things Nigel finds polluting. He requires all to relieve themselves of these demonic influences before any can enter his mansion. I complied.

Nigel's mansion turns out to be the building that housed his formerly prosperous clothing boutique which catered to the sartorial demands of the Jamaican elite. The quarters are large, two stories high, with spacious rooms that are now bereft of furniture and decoration. Nigel's mansion is but a vestige of the glamour and prestige he enjoyed as one of the wealthiest tailors in Jamaica. The yellow clippings that hang willy-nilly from the flaking walls of the main room bear silent witness to Nigel's renunciation of both his business and family. The Jamaican media once celebrated him as a promising designer of clothes for both the wealthy and the celebrated. That was before his commitment to the principles of Rastafari.

Nigel explains his conversion to Rastafari as an odyssey, a passage that began shortly after his appendectomy operation. Then modern drugs and treatments were of no avail in restoring his energy, vitality and spirit. However, an encounter with a Rasta turned into meetings of mutual communication and disclosure. On the Rasta's advice, Nigel drank large amounts of ganja tea and smoked equally large amounts of marijuana. He recovered his health. From then on, he affiliated himself with the ways of Rastafari, and he too hallowed the herb as the healing of nations. Furthermore, he attributes the restoration and continuance of his health to his dedication to the Rasta principles of love, meditation, reasoning and ital (natural) foods of which marijuana is a part.

Nigel found peace when he embraced Rastafari. His fashion industry and family were the weapons he created to wage warfare on people. Thus, he divested himself of his career and married life.

Shortly after his conversion in 1981, Nigel began to send funds to Rastas in the rural interior. At that time, Jamaican businesses were recouping their losses suffered under the democratic socialism of the Manley government which had threatened their profits. Nigel recalls how the bank officials thought that he was donating funds to a subversive group in the interior. A popular rumor at the time was that Manley's allies had contingents ready in the country who would help Cuban communists infiltrate Jamaica. Nigel was under great suspicion. The bank refused to handle any of his transactions. The government harassed him on charges of tax evasion. His wife tried to commit him to a mental institution. Nigel muses: "Because I was becoming aware of my own identity, I had to go through this suffering. That's in the past, the price I paid. Now I am free."

Now Nigel is neither an entrepreneur nor an artist but an ascetic. He refuses to touch money, and only the free will offerings of others sustain him. His meatless diet consists only of fruits, vegetables and an occasional fish. He abhors the eating of animal meat because dead flesh will only cause sickness for the person who consumes it. Nor will he accept any fruit or vegetable whose natural appearance has been altered by any cutting, mashing or peeling. Nigel seems lanky and anorexic. However, his appearance belies his vigor and vitality which are evident in his darting about and enthusiastically engaging the visitor in philosophical discussion about the affairs of the world, the way to health and the meaning of sexuality.

Rastas such as Nigel and this brother identify with Haile Selassie as the Conquering Lion of Judah. (William Lewis)

An aroma of ganja smoke clings to Nigel's long, unkempt and natural dreads. This slovenliness too is deceptive because Nigel is particularly fastidious about the cleanliness of his body and he meticulously monitors its functions. This leads him to administer frequent purgatives to himself lest the accumulation of toxins within cause harm for the whole body. His frequent cleansings and purgations of the body as well as the avoidance of contact with any decaying matter, especially a dead body, are normative in Nigel's life. Were these norms violated, his spiritual and physical health would be imperiled.

Without his regimen, Nigel would be unable to find the strength to weave his philosophical reflections through his writings, his conversations and solitary moments of meditation. Esoteric writings and volumes are scattered throughout his quarters. He has amassed stacks of newspaper clippings and sundry writings whose relationship to the philosophy of Rastafari at first glance appears obscure. Nevertheless, Nigel can explain every metaphor and symbol in his literary collection and connect them to what he believes are the truths of Rastafari. Included in his assemblage of works are titles such as: "Dread Locks Judgement," "Anthropology: Races of Man," "Radical Vegetarianism," "Rasta Voice Magazine," "Economy and Business," "Women as Sex Object," and "Pan African Digest." His own essays range from glosses on Joseph Owens' *Dread* and Dennis Forsythe's *Healing of Nations* to highly idealistic writing on a new economic order. Among these pieces is correspondence from previous English and American visitors to Nigel's mansion.

Nigel's own writings have an intense and highly involuted style which gives them an arcane quality, a form somewhat reminiscent of James Joyce's stream of consciousness. Tolerance and patience are demanded of the reader who wishes to decipher Nigel's turn of phrase and novel transformation of words. Indeed, the uninitiated reader might wonder if the police are not correct in simply shrugging him off as a Rasta who has had too much ganja. His prose is obscure and agonistic, but, nevertheless, he can elicit sense from every syllable, word and line. Nigel's deftness in turning his twisted writings into an articulate message makes him a shaman and mythmaker of sorts, for his vocalizations about the revelation he bears have the rhythm, cadence and timbre of a person standing outside of the self.

A passage from his political and social writings reads:

> This will be conceder as the first in a seerie of poblishing that wil be for propor translactions of internatciall master in the

Civitas Dei Epich Poblishing. One will find a presen the banking and insurance brokerages international are controlled by I.C.A. and K.B.G. This situactions is monapolized by neocoloialization a-liances accocations. Their names are too numberous to menation at this time as I would not have enough paper to do so. So the anatics will be done in brief. The concet of escange of goods and services condemns the capitalistic and that is in fact criminal in the final analesis an immoral item that offends the Civitas Dei in principle.

In discussing this passage with Nigel, I learned that his concept of "Civitas Dei" (City of God) is the Rastas' theocratic government that Nigel finds at the core of enlightenment. He dismisses the democratic administration in Jamaica as the work of demons and delights in pointing out how the prefix *dem* appears in both demon and democracy. Following this penchant which is common among Rastas, Nigel can whittle down a word and cull from it a hidden meaning. Rather than democracy, Nigel calls for a theocracy based on God's justice and disarmament. This is the people's government that flourishes in the interior sections of Jamaica where Rastas pursue their lives independent of city businesses. Nigel wants this theocracy transposed to an urban environment where it would enhance the medical, religious, sexual and political dimensions of the person. Only then will people be free to exchange goods and services in a moral way without the interference of an outside power or democracy.

The Upper Room

Nigel's "Upper Room" is on the second level of the building with two large windows opening to a view of eastern Kingston and allowing the cool breezes from the sea to circulate through the room. It is furnished with a few mats, a raggedy sleeping cot over to the side, a square table on which the herb is blessed, and shelves along the wall on which lie chillum pipes of various lengths. The chillum pipes are stored for other Rastas who might visit and join Nigel for reasoning. In his Upper Room Nigel undergoes his most intense experience with ganja and elaborates ecstatically on Rastafari. In accord with what he believes to be Rastas' tradition, he excludes women from these sessions.

When the brethren have gathered in the Upper Room, Nigel raises his arms toward the East in a grand gesture and blesses the herb with vocalizations resembling glossolalia. "Amharic," he says as an aside, "the Ethiopian language." The blessings are spontaneous and ecstatic, but on listening closely I detected a word that sounded like *mirrikat*, the Amharic word for blessing. Later Nigel mentioned that he learned some Amharic at the Ethiopian Orthodox Church in Kingston.

After the chillum is filled, and the herb is burning, Nigel is the first to draw deeply from the pipe. His chest expands as smoke fills his lungs. He exhales billows of smoke through his nostrils and mouth, and the whiffs frame his lionlike face with tendrils of plumes that seep through his long locks and beard. Through the clouds of smoke, Nigel stares at all in the room with a fierce look, regal, but cutting and penetrating. His demeanor demands a response.

"The conquering Lion of Judah shall break every chain," I acclaim.

Nigel seems pleased with this affirmation of his link with the Emperor Haile Selassie, the Lion of Judah.

Another's turn comes to partake of the chalice, and Nigel passes the pipe with a most respectful gesture. Kneeling before the next brother with his own head bowed low to the floor, his outstretched arms offer him the chillum. The brother accepts, draws from it, and proclaims, "Jah Rastafari."

The chillum moves from participant to participant, brother to brother, each honoring the other with gestures of deference but never permitting their flesh to meet. Bodily contact is assiduously avoided. Soon the participants assume unusual bodily postures. The effect is startling. Nigel takes the lead in displaying great physical agility and dexterity by twisting his body into yogalike positions. All the brethren follow suit. They throw their bodies into lionlike leaps. Nevertheless, their bodily deportments are undertaken with great concentration and awareness, for not once did their acrobatic feats threaten to harm anyone in the room.

"What is love?" asks one of the brothers.

"Love is where there are no starving people. As long as there are hungry people, hatred is in power. Caring and supporting . . ."

Their dance continues, and perhaps ten minutes passes.

"Sex is a performance, a duty."

"Women are for pickneys (babies)."

Another interval, and more of their dancing.

"Burn Babylon." Some begin chanting the familiar lyric.

"Why the police brutality and why youths beaten by Babylon? They steal because they are hungry and want to fill their bellies. No crime in taking food because you are hungry."

"Africa for the blacks, Europe for the whites, Jamaica for the Arawaks."

I ask, "Where does all your wisdom come from?"

And the five respond in antiphonal style.

"It comes from inside."

"My surroundings and nature. I sense everything."

"Everything."

"Inside."

"Rasta knowledge comes from a free consciousness, heart. It comes from here (pointing toward the heart) and not from books."

Throughout the night the session reviews the same issues of knowledge, wisdom and peace, drawing them together in the fashion of pointillism. It is always the mind that must see the connection. Toward midnight, one of the brethren takes a small drum from the shelf and taps out a beat with the refrain:

"Nyabinghy."

And another adds: "Man—earth."

"Nyabinghy."

"Man—earth."

"Nyabinghy."

The next day I set out to meet David and Lion.

David and Lion

Tourists and Jamaicans alike must cross an unsteady, wooden pier in order to board the ferry that takes passengers from Kingston Harbor to the legendary Port Royal across the bay. Once celebrated as a haunt for pirates and a playground for debauchery, Port Royal now rests quietly on the bay, chastised forever, it seems, by the raging earthquake it suffered in the late seventeenth century. That cataclysm hurled much of the port into the Caribbean.

Near the ramp leading to the pier lazes David, a Rasta brother. He is attending his concession stand which is simply a large crate hoisted on a dolly for maneuverability. From the cart, David sells Red Stripe beer, D & G sodas, as well as Benson cigarettes by ones and twos, and, of course, raw sugar cane and coconut, the most popular items. A sampling from his assortment of refreshments often comes as welcome relief for the overheated traveler after the half-hour trip across the bay.

David and Lion live together in a hovel about twenty yards from their stand. The shack rests precariously on the side of the pier, supported in part by the hanging branches of a huge tree on which part of it also leans. The roof and sidings are constructed of huge pieces of cardboard and plastic sheeting. Nearby, a slipshod folding chair, unworthy of any task, clings to the pier's edge and marks out an area that serves as a reception space for guests. The sound

Homemade shacks selling Rasta foods are common in Jamaica and Barbados. (Richard Kenefick)

of the rushing water against the piles, the squeaking of the rats, and the dust from the parched earth fill the place David and Lion call home with a romantic irony. They sit between two worlds, perhaps a sign of their liminality. From one viewpoint, Port Royal's outlines loom across the bay standing witness to wanton living long ago. From another angle stands the symbol of law and order, a police station, to which the Rastas pay no heed.

Lion and David eat *ital* food, a healthy low-salt, low-fat and low-cholesterol diet, that consists mainly of vegetables, plantains and the occasional red snapper, caught off the pier. At a clearing away from their hut, they prepare the food on an aluminum can cover some twenty-four inches in diameter. The fare is seasoned with hot pepper and served on tin plates. Sometimes a rat might boldly rush a dish at what appears to be an opportune moment in an effort to wrest a morsel from a distracted diner. The Rastas, however, are generous and share their food with any of their guests, human and animal alike.

When business is slow at their stand, Lion, David and other brethren hustle on the streets of Kingston, selling anything from boxed donuts to belts and tams (knitted headgear which they themselves have crafted). They are talkative entrepreneurs and quick to prevail upon a prospective customer, especially a white tourist, to purchase one of their handiworks or products.

Reasoning

Toward late afternoon on a hot July day, two brethren arrive at the pier and exchange greetings with David. David assures the visiting brethren that I, the white guest sitting near the hut, have respect and love for Rastafari. Lion emerges from below the rafters of the pier where he was resting and lends support to David's assurances that their white visitor is trustworthy.

When the group is ready, David places the Bible on the ground and marks off a few pages from which he will draw his inspiration. The spliffs are lit with a short grace: "Give thanks." At that moment, however, some youths happen on the scene, probably drawn by the whiff of ganja smoke overcoming the salty sea breezes. They ask for some herb. Lion rebukes the boys and says: "This is high reasoning, boys, and not play." They run off. The Rastas return to the matter at hand.

David mulls over the scriptural passage about the Nazarites and the proscription on the cutting of hair. "Love is the foundation of Rastafari. The covenant is the hair, the locks. This is Godly."

As a group of commuters disembarks from the ferry and hurries by the group, scarcely giving them a glance, Lion comments: "Jamaican people cannot see the truth. They have eyes, hands, feet, but don't use them properly for justice and love. They are blinded."

Rashi holds his spliff and remarks pensively: "Rastas are clever, living for truth. The weed is important. It is healing."

After reflecting a bit on the wisdom in the herb, the Rastas turn to excoriating the success of reggae musicians, a discussion that enlivens the group. Few endearing words are spent on reggae musicians who, the Rastas believe, preach the philosophy of Rastafari, give interviews to magazines, enrich themselves, but filter none of their profits into the creation of a stronger culture for the rest of the brethren.

"Look how they draw up around Nesta's place on New Hope, clean and shining. Burn reggae."

All agree.

Soon the brethren fall into a quiet, meditative mood. A few reflect in low voices on the similarity between the churches and reggae. This prompts David to take up a verse from the scriptures and freely elaborate on it. The verse is: "Let the dead bury the dead."

"The churches in Jamaica bury only dead people, and take people's money to build bigger church buildings, instead of providing work and industry for people. The Rasta never dies but has life eternal, as Christ promised. God cannot lie. To have life eternal one must follow the Rasta culture in the Bible. Rasta is a new name. It is the new Jerusalem that Isaiah promised in the prophecy."

David's words excite the group, and they all affirm the equality of people. They denounce the hypocrisy of organized religion, reggae and the government for manipulating the Bible and authority. The more their anger with society increases, so much the more does the spontaneity of the gathering quicken.

David takes the spliff from a Rasta reclining next to him. Holding it, he prays that the chalice be not a source of condemnation but a guardian of life eternal. He inhales deeply, holds the smoke within, and for almost a minute after exhalation he gazes intently on me, the white visitor sitting across from him. Then:

"Rasta is not the color of the skin. Blacks hate their fellow man, just like white man hates. Even some Rastas have words on their lips but not in their hearts."

As darkness draws closer, and fewer people queue up for the ferry, the Rastas become more vociferous.

"Living is for the Rastas. Moses and the prophets are not dead, but reign in Zion, a Kingdom that is better than the one here. I have life. I will never die but go to Zion with Ras Tafari Selassie I" [pronounced as "aye"].

Interspersed among their exultations of Selassie are monotone chantings expressing a yearning for repatriation to a land of freedom from which they have been exiled.

"Africa yes! But not the Africa of today because it is just as corrupt as Jamaica."

Silence. The spliffs are lit again, passed around and blessed. The mood changes. The brethren become serious and playful, ecstatic and earthly. Lion leads this flow of sensuousness. He rolls on the ground, smiles, laughs lightly while singing an improvisation on liberty, freedom and repatriation. He kisses the roots of a nearby tree and exclaims: "Jah Rastafari."

The others participate in his display with their own paeans on liberation and freedom. Soon they too tumble over the ground, enjoying themselves immensely, and encouraging me to "ride the vibes and feel freedom."

At dusk, bright lights illumine the decks of a British warship that had docked in the harbor earlier in the day. The sharp relief of the ship in the distance prompts Lion to remark:

"War is against Rastafari. Rastas do what is right for life and live forever. Jamaican people love war too much. I don't know why."

David pursues the thought further. "I-n-I is never listened to. We are rejected. They have no culture. They steal, kill and shoot."

Lion snuggles closer to the roots of the tree which are bulging from the parched earth. He seems to caress them.

"I-n-I Rastafari are the love in the world. We are very peaceful, loving and don't eat poisonous things, no salt, no liver, no dead animals."

Rashi adds: "We want wholeness, fullness of justice, fullness of love."

When asked to identify the source of his power, Rashi responds:

"I-n-I is the bible in the heart. The true bible is yet to be written. I-n-I moves beyond the bible. It is a word that we must move beyond. I-n-I live naturally in the fullness of divinity, don't have to go to school. Truth is in the heart. I-n-I have to learn our flesh and blood. Then everybody gets food, shelter. This is the truth."

Popes and priests irritate them. "Burn the pope. Burn the pope man. The Church is a vampire with their cars and living in the hills [an area where the elite reside]. The pope is a vampire, wants our blood. Selassie I is the head. The pope is the devil."

The light fades. More silence. The bay water slaps against the pilings. A rat tears across the planks and startles me. I jump. Lion, however, admonishes me with a reminder that the rat is only a creature.

"The barber shop is the mark of the beast. Comb and razor conquer. The wealth of Jah is with locks, in fullness of his company."

All nod in agreement. I mention that my understanding is increasing.

"Be careful with words, brother," Lion says, "overstand not understand. I people are forward people not backward."

Another interjects: "It is a brand new way of life. The language of I-n-I is forward. I-n-I people will pay no more. For five hundred years, they built Babylon on us, but they will do it no more."

Across the bay the lights from Port Royal flicker. An Air Jamaica flight readies for its landing and swoops low over the waters. Then Lion rises and stretches his arms toward Port Royal.

"Judgment of Jah is severe. He destroyed the pirates over in Port Royal with the great earthquake. He will destroy those who do not follow I with nuclear weapons from the sky."

Then David: "World War III is the judgment. But I-n-I is not afraid of nuclear weapons. We are one people. We deal in the living."

Darkness finally envelops the group. A small fire soon blazes into a roar. The squeaking of the rats and the salty smells of the bay give way to the scents of burning wood and the crackling of cardboard and paper. Then all chant their monotone verses over and over again, some with expressions so arcane that they defy translation except for a sprinkling of words such as freedom and repatriation. The brethren say they speak in Amharic, the language of Ethiopia, and among their words I catch "tiru, tiru" which in Amharic means "nice."

Eventually all fall asleep. At daybreak, each rises, bathes in the waters, washes his clothes, dries them in the morning sun, and then goes on his way to hustle, to seek the companionship of other Rastas and share whatever each might have to divide with the other. David leaves the pier grounds to visit Rastas further in the city. From them he will purchase the gum, candies, cigarettes and beer that are the primary stock on his stand.

"Praise Jah. Selassie I. One love." A biscuit and ganja tea start the day.

A return visit a week later finds Lion lying alone on the scorched earth. Another Rasta joins him. Lion speaks in ponderous tones, neither excited nor vindictive.

"David cut I-n-I up and stole I-n-I money. He has Rasta on his lips, but not in his heart. I-n-I is at peace. Let the dead bury the dead."

Later I learned that David received a just recompense for his untoward behavior against Lion. The uptown brethren beat him severely when his deed was brought to their attention. The local police did not interfere with this administration of Rastas' justice, even though David was close to death due to the beatings he received.

4

Rastas in a Kingston Suburb

Pierport is a respectable middle class housing development and suburb a few miles to the west of the heart of downtown Kingston. A causeway links the suburban community, built on reclaimed marsh lands, with the Kingston metropolis. Lloyd and Gordon are Rastas in their early twenties who live here with their wives and children. They follow the tenets of Rastafari but do so in an economic and symbolic context that differentiates them from Lion, Nigel and the Rastas at the beach.

Pierport

Pierport's residents have status. Its population comes from the teaching profession, the civil service, the blue-collar industrial sector of the economy, and small scale entrepreneurs such as tailors, small shop owners, and families who own the buses and vans that transport passengers to and from Kingston. Their claim to privilege and respectability is not simply based on economic matters, for status differentiation involves other issues, such as the appearance of their homes, their manner of expressing religion, their civic mindedness, and the separation between the male and female spheres of influence.

Pierport's housing stock contrasts dramatically with the homes of the lower classes, who are scattered in hamlets and lanes on the periphery of the suburb. The "sufferahs'" houses do not exhibit the veranda, the manicured gardens, the walled-in enclosures, private baths, modern kitchens, plumbing and the other amenities of the privileged classes such as the telephone, the television and easy access to public transportation. The lesser status of the poor shows itself in zinc roofing, outside sinks, chickens and goats meandering through the yard and the house, poor sewerage, if any, and no garbage collections by a city agency. The poor are left to their own ingenious devices.

The middle class of Pierport shares an assumption with the elite who reside in the hilly slopes north of Kingston and whose night lights are clearly visible to the residents of Pierport below. Both hold that the lower classes are responsible for their inferior position because of their cultural ways. The poor are not educated, express no sobriety in their religious ecstasy, are lax in female chastity, enjoy ganja too frequently and unreservedly, and have no political mind. This is a class bias that is shared by the Jamaican middle class whenever it reflects on the status of the lower classes.

Pierport is a Christian community. The religious effervescence of the believers, however, is controlled, and the residents frown upon any manifestation of spirit possession and trance during religious services. The Christian denominations, Roman Catholic, Episcopal, Methodist and Evangelical, enjoy ecumenical relations on occasion by joining together for prayerful assembly. The Seventh Day Adventists and Jehovah's Witnesses, however, shy away from such conviviality because they do not approve of the other churches' laxity evident by their toleration of alcoholic beverages and tobacco. Periodically, however, all the churches sponsor meetings that draw the residents together for discussion about issues that concern the whole community, for instance, the problem of drugs, the building of a community center, and the removal of trash.

No one in Pierport claims to be a root person or folk healer. Nor does anyone practice obeah, or witchcraft, which is illegal in Jamaica. These are the "superstitions" of the lower classes who believe that "duppies," or spirits of the recently deceased, come from the woods at night to haunt the hapless living. Yet, in spite of its disdain for the customs of the lower classes, Pierport does have its unemployed who manage to survive on the good will offerings of their relatives or else hustle a living through illegal gambling activities and the ganja traffic.

In Pierport, symbolic means of differentiation are more prominent than economic ones. The residents sport expensive cars, but they may leave them idle in the carports because of lack of funds for petrol. They may conspicuously display television dish antennas on their roofs, but many also have their electricity and water cut off due to failure to pay the bills. Nevertheless, the symbols of status remain in spite of economic difficulties. Economic strain on the community does not affect the status to which they claim a title. Values, morals and the symbols of affluence seem to have as much or more to do with their sense of superior status than does the economic issue of income distribution, a private matter and well-guarded secret in the community. One gets the impression that the flow of money in Pierport is due to other factors than the legitimate market economy.

Respectability and Role

Distinctive male and female roles underlie the symbolic world of Pierport, the former revolving around economic issues and the latter around morals.

A Jamaican middle-class woman maintains her respectability in the community by belonging to an organized church. Indeed, women comprise the greater part of church membership in Pierport. Even though the male clergy upbraid the men with scriptural chapter and verse for failing to take up their Christian responsibility and join the churches, this is of no avail. Men simply believe that churchgoing is the woman's role.

Beyond the church, a woman's respectability depends upon her married state, or at least a stable live-in union. Her reputation depends on her maintenance of a clean home and her watchfulness over immaculately groomed children who are never to go without shoes. The older women eagerly guard the standards of respectability in Pierport through their networks of gossip. Their biting words circulate throughout the community constantly and review the credentials of this or that woman's claim to respectability.

At community meetings the women are the most vocal in demanding better police protection against theft, more bus stops, improved lighting, frequent garbage collections, adequate health facilities and a staffed counselling center for family planning. Men, of course, will participate in these discussions, but the women take the lead, and the men feign enthusiasm. Their concerns lie elsewhere, with economics and patronage.

The women are the gatekeepers of cultural values and norms, but this is not without its tensions, as the following incident demonstrates. At an ecumenical church meeting, moral questions were raised about dishonesty, theft and ganja dealing. The women pointed out that villainy was becoming respectable in Jamaican life.

They bolstered their complaint with a deliberate aside on the illegal activities of some of the men, e.g., gambling and the ganja trade. The men rejoined that Jamaicans were living far beyond their means and that too much money was spent on sending children abroad to pursue higher standards of living when they should remain at home. The men placed much of the blame for this state of affairs on the women. In response, the women reminded the men that they, the women, were the ones who kept the houses neat, the children clean, and added that they were not philandering around town. The entire exchange that evening pointed out the expectations each had of the other.

The woman's primary responsibility is to maintain the integrity of the family. The husband may be a drunkard and ne'er-do-well, but she must uphold the honor of the household through her virtuous life. She must abstain from alcoholic beverages and engage in no sexual liaisons, as far as public knowledge can gather. She may even take up employment. For her courage and fortitude, she receives the admiration of her fellow church members, the respect of her children and the praise coming from the local gossip circuits. When necessary, church members will come to her aid with food and money, impressed as they are with her diligent and virtuous life.

Incidents such as the following exemplify the central position of respect that the woman commands in her family. An errant son had not reported home after a few days' jaunt in Kingston. Fears mounted that he might have become involved in the drug business, an occupation for which his youth and naivete did not suit him. When a neighbor spotted him on the streets of Kingston and called the family to inform them of his whereabouts, his mother's remarks to the caller were: "Tell him to remember his mother." This sentiment, the mother believed, would bring the son home. He returned that evening.

The men have different responsibilities. They spend most of their day building up networks that center around the possibility of getting a job, keeping it and advancing to a better economic position. Theirs is the world of patronage. After working hours the men are likely to spend some time in the bars and clubs located in the fashionable areas of Kingston where they can socialize with influential people. This helps them expand the opportunities for cultivating networks that might lead to fraternity with the Jamaican elite and their economic favors.

The men do not guard the moral sphere with the intensity of the women, especially in the area of sexuality. For instance, a woman may be aware of her husband's amorous adventures with other women but seldom, if ever, take any action against him. Chastity, however, is demanded of the female.

The Italian expression *bella figura*, which means "a good appearance," best summarizes Pierport's moral demeanor. Pierport's residents are willing to tolerate private breaches of the code as long as the appearances of respectability are maintained. They can even ignore the "weakness of the flesh" in their clergy's dalliances provided they fulfill their public role as helpers of people. Homosexuality is a taboo topic among men, and stories abound of male homosexuals who suffer cruel punishments for their sexual behavior at the hands of mobs who stone them. However, some married men are not daunted by such tales and keep male lovers in secret while maintaining a family. Their conduct causes no commotion, provided, of course, the man is not effeminate, and does not flaunt his sexuality in open defiance of the public code. If the man fulfills his role as father and worker, little will be said, and seldom is his sexuality a matter for public discussion. When the topic is raised in public, and a person is accused of homosexual activity, the charge is denied by the parties concerned, and that generally closes the case.

A man's reputation in Pierport is based on his economic role, and the woman's on her morality. Rule bending and adjustments are made, but this never occurs in the public realm of social discourse, only in the private sphere of clandestine activity. In the public sphere, morality, reputation, and respectability are defended by both men and women alike.

The middle class of Pierport, then, is not a world solely described in terms of economic categories. Jamaicans attach great significance to other means of differentiation such as whether or not one has an education, whether or not one's children walk about with shoes on their feet, whether or not one attends a refined church, i.e., a church that does not encourage the possession trance. Indeed, Pierport residents place a great significance on the nonmaterialistic aspects of life, and these play as much a role in their claim to status and respectability as any economic factor. This is truly "bella figura."

Lloyd and Gordon

Lloyd works as a trucker and transports produce to the food markets on the north coast and to the markets in the Kingston area. He wears his hair in dreads, sometimes covering them with a knitted tam accented by the red, green and gold of African patriotism. When not working, he enjoys cycling around the neighborhood, chatting with friends and acquaintances, and playing football. He has a wife, and his two young daughters attend a licensed school.

Gordon does not wear his hair in dreads, seldom plays football and has a position as a teller in the Bank of Nova Scotia in Kingston. His home is not as spacious as Lloyd's, a two story dwelling with a veranda overlooking the bay.

Gordon and Lloyd often reason with other Rastas from the neighborhood and often invite the young members of the local PNP organization to join them. The preferred setting for their convivial sessions is usually Lloyd's veranda, cooled by the night breezes from the bay while all stretch out on lounge chairs, shirtless and in summer shorts. On a warm evening in August, Gordon, Lloyd and others gathered together to reason about the meaning of Rastafari. I accepted the invitation to join them. Our reflections focused on a wide range of topics, including Selassie I, sexuality, ganja and politics.

Lloyd began the reasoning session by citing legends about Ethiopia's greatness, Selassie's repulsion of Mussolini's invading troops, and the address that Selassie delivered to the League of Nations. His paean was filled with tales about Selassie's generosity to the poor, his ability to read the hearts and minds of men, and his possession of the sacred ring of Solomon. (Legend has it that an Ethiopian prince who fled to the United States after the deposition of Selassie in 1974 gave it to Bob Marley during one of his tours. After Marley's death, the ring was not seen, if, indeed, the ring he wore was truly the one belonging to Selassie I.) Ideas about freedom, repatriation and a new world dominated Lloyd's vision which he centered on the person of Selassie I. He explained how Selassie directed the world toward peace, but sadly his admonitions were never heeded. Selassie was a figure of mythic proportions for Lloyd, and his unknown place of burial gave cause for wonder on whether he was really dead.

"When His Imperial Majesty was crowned, all kinds of supernatural signs surrounded him. His Imperial Majesty has the same roots as Jesus Christ. Just as Christ incarnated divinity in his day, so His Imperial Majesty did it again for our day. Some people worship His Imperial Majesty as God, some as a King, some as a King and a God.

"I was changed to Rastafari because I am a black man. Rastafari is a sweet concept, a living up to a certain standard. I'm happy that I've found the truth. Some people are still searching for it. Open heart and open mind."

After Lloyd mused on the meaning of Selassie and the grounds for his conversion to Rastafari, Gordon continued:

"The whole message of Rastafari is contained in the Book of Revelations. In the United States, the evangelist Herbert Armstrong interprets the Bible just as the Rastas do."

On the identity of God, Gordon offered this notion: "God can be known and seen. He is the King from the line of Judah."

When I suggested that Haile was dead, he responded: "The tomb was left vacant. But he will return."

Gordon freely used Christian imagery to sustain his belief in Rastafari by alluding to Herbert Armstrong, and Scriptural references to Jesus, such as the story of the empty tomb, were applied to Haile Selassie. The source for these orthodox Christian references was probably the influence of the Ethiopian Orthodox Church in Kingston, established in 1969 after Selassie's visit to Jamaica. Many Rastas in Pierport attended the liturgical services there but on an infrequent basis.

Soon the discussion turned toward women and sexuality. The subject was sparked by Lloyd's wife who brought in the fruit drinks for the guests. After serving them, she retired to another room, a common practice among Jamaican women when their husbands are entertaining male guests.

Lloyd stated: "A woman's role is not the man's role."

A PNP member mentioned that some Jamaican women are so sensitive to the lack of interest that Rasta men display toward women that they say the Rastas are "boddy" (gay) men. Everyone smiled and then burst into laughter.

Gordon interrupted the hilarity with great indignation and explained that women are a necessary component to complete his masculinity. He held that women must be subservient to men. The biblical Adam, he believed, was the first creation and this alone justifies the males' rights over females.

Homosexuality received scant attention, but the topic bothered Gordon more than the others. Lloyd was not upset by the idea, provided the person was not forced into the role. Nevertheless, Lloyd notes that certain acts between men such as sodomy and fellation were reprehensible in the sight of Jah. Yet, both he and Gordon understood how homosexuality could increase in the cities because of economic reasons. They ascribed the rise in it to the need for making a living. The latter point, which reduces homosexual activity to economic undercurrents, received a nod of approval from all.

Questions about sexuality do not interest the group as much as Lloyd's contrast of Rastafari with the possession religions that are

common in Jamaica. For Lloyd, Rasta is sweetness, and not the
terrifying paroxysms of trance so common among the poor. Lloyd
has a particular dislike for the Pocomanians, a possession religion
whose members, he believes, persuaded the police to destroy the
Rastas commune at the Pinnacle in the 1950s because of their
jealousy over the Rastas' ability to attract the poor.

Possession by spirits turned into a discussion of the Kingdom of
Satan and evil. Gordon took the lead.

"Nuclear weapons, including Russia's, are not fulfilling the Bible's
prediction that the mountains will cover the people up when the
world ends. The United States and Russia have built huge cities
to hide from the bomb, but God will send earthquakes to destroy
them. God will destroy the world by fire, nuclear fire."

Gordon used apocalyptic imagery to describe the demise of
Babylon, the Kingdom of Satan, and the rise of the Kingdom of God.
This was a rhetoric familiar enough in Pierport, for it was used by
the prominent Adventist Churches. Gordon saw the universe
evolving under the guidance of God. The outcome of the process
was not in the hands of man.

"The Kingdom of God will come about without man's help
because it is a law that God has put into the universe. If one
discovers the mind of God, one can see God's plan unfolding."

Babylon has power, but about it Gordon says:

"Babylon is so powerful because it is a kingdom that has many
friends. It is built on lies, and the truth has many enemies."

Gordon takes the Pope as the enemy, the incarnation of Satan,
a common belief also among some of the Adventist churches. This
is a repetition of the scorn and derision that the Twelve Tribers in
Kingston heap upon the Pope, priests and others. Gordon believes
that an essential truth of Rastafari is that the Roman Church is
Satan.

Lloyd had some reservations about Gordon's rhetoric. "But why
would a man become a Rasta if not to better his life here? Rastas
do not believe in another world but the belief is here."

Interestingly, no one is smoking the herb during the reasoning
session. Everyone agrees that the herb should be used in private,
alone and behind closed doors. Do not the scriptures say that one
should go behind closed doors when praying? Commenting upon
its use by the non-Rastas, Lloyd says: "The herb doesn't work for
the selfish people of Babylon in the way it is supposed to work."

Lloyd liked to describe his commitment to Rastafari as a sweet
thing, and the smoking of the herb brought sweetness.

"Smoking constantly keeps your mind going. That's what it does.

Rastas meld biblical themes such as the Last Supper with their own symbols. (Richard Kenefick)

You can use the herb in other ways besides smoking, if it's too much for you, like in a drink. This is good."

He pointed to his heart, breast and thighs, expressing the sweetness within. Then, he continued:

"Babylon persecutes the herb. But people need the herb to slow down and find peace. People move too fast."

A question befuddled the group. It concerned the possibility of a political group manipulating the symbols of Rastafari. Soon they arrived at an answer. All agreed that the Jamaican Labor Party and the Workers' Party of Jamaica were parties that manipulate Rasta because Washington and Moscow controlled both of them, the former capitalist and the latter socialist. However, they praise the People's National Party because it upheld black self-worth and agitated for the people's interests rather than for those of outsiders. They were Manley sympathizers.

The group held that ganja and politics do not mix. Lloyd said that he would never campaign for the legalization of marijuana in any way "because the political programs of the JLP are really dirty in Jamaica with violence and all."

In spite of this, both Lloyd and Gordon understood the reasons for the dealing in marijuana. As Lloyd explained it:

"What is wrong with making extra money from the sale of the herb? The Jamaican economy cannot support us."

Gordon and Lloyd expressed a great interest in the organizations of Rastafari. Gordon used the Twelve Tribes in Kingston as an example of a group which gave to Rastafari a sense of identity that was comparable to that of the churches. Organization allowed the Rastas to accomplish their goals. The PNP members attending the session quickly pursued the point and used it to advocate the need for Rastas to cooperate with the PNP.

Into the evening, the discussion grew old by turning and returning to the sweetness of Rastafari, its liberation of mind and body, its manifestation of God's power and its awareness of God's design in human history. Relaxed and comfortable, I too believed it all.

5

Commentary

Lion, Nigel and the Rastas at the beach have created a cultural context which breaks down the social discourse of modern society. Social discourse is understood here as the pattern of role and status accepted as the legal and political norms of the dominant society. The linkage of role, status and power is not only ideological but the very substance of institutions such as the family, correctional facilities, and the police. This structure, however, can be undermined through resistance that interferes with the reproduction of social institutions. The Rastas resist social discourse, for example, by refusing to vote, to join the army, and to work for tax paying businesses. Instead of wage labor, they favor independent occupations like fishing, handicrafts, ganja trading and general hustling. Their occupations indicate that they labor outside of the market economy. In their activities, they struggle not only to reappropriate for themselves a material basis for production but also to establish new relationships between individuals in their daily lives.

The Rastas' economic patterns prevent any of their enterprises from matching the productivity and profits of the bourgeois world. Their symbolic world sustains an economic system that impedes the development of those structures that modern society deems rational and necessary for the accumulation of wealth. In their outlook and value system, the Rastas are antimodern. The Rastas at the beach, for example, impede the growth of economic profits by squatting on valuable beachfront lands as if they were the gift of Haile Selassie. For them, the symbolic value of the land supersedes its economic potential. They do not subscribe to the plans of the Urban Development Corporation and its view that development of the land will mean progress for the Rastas as well as the rest of society. Nigel renounces worldly pursuits with such feverish intensity that some take him to be mad. Lion pursues an undisciplined life which leads to chicanery and rowdiness of all kinds, unfavorable traits for economic growth.

The Rastas' separatism has distanced them from Jamaican religious practices, insulated them from the medical warnings about marijuana and desensitized them to the propaganda for economic progress. In other words, the Rastas have withdrawn materialistically and symbolically from the interests that motivate a class-based society. The creation of a boundary between themselves and the rest of society is the foundation from which the Rastas construct their social body, a common strategy for the development of social consciousness in any group.

Economics, Modernity and Religion

Nigel epitomizes the person who resists performing mechanically "in work or love" according to the dictates of a secular society. He will not permit himself to be reduced occupationally or emotionally by conventional society's view of what is rational. Nigel creates a new text which he uses to interpret, fashion, and construct a meaningful world. His repudiation of his former career and his embrace of celibacy, vegetarianism and arcane patterns of speech and writing are expressions of his commitment to Rastafari. He has ignored the medical profession's pronouncements on marijuana, society's expectations of male sexuality, and the authority of the established churches. He has even managed to unravel the psychological meanings of sexuality by dismissing the importance of female sexuality in a man's life, truly an anomaly for the Jamaican male. Together with his friends, Nigel luxuriates in the male world as they dance out the ecstatic mime that takes hold of them during their reasoning sessions. A celebration of the body is a social text for many Rastas.

Lion and his friends also live in a world which does not attach any normative significance to the warnings about marijuana, the praises heaped upon the nuclear family and the glorification of the accumulation of wealth. While they are not world renouncers who await redemption after death, their survival depends very little on the standards of the dominant society. Not only do they reject bourgeois morality, they sympathize with those who make their way in life without succumbing to the seduction of bourgeois society. Their moral tolerance allows them to embrace the brigands of society. Yet their indifference to the niceties of society does not make Lion and his friends ripe for membership in profitable crime syndicates. Those in organized crime tend to accumulate more wealth and power in the ganja trade than do Rastas. The economic activities surrounding the use and sale of ganja among the Rastas are grounded in the community's flows of gossip, sexual liaisons, and reasoning sessions. These elements can intrude into a Rasta economic enterprise at any given moment to stymie plans that would increase individual profit.

In an angry rage over an unfaithful woman, for instance, one Rasta at the beach plowed under a field of marijuana, burnt the stock in a bonfire, and hurled the ashes into the sea. The very expressions that provide for communal integration, namely, the outbursts of passionate redress against an offender of their norms, also prevent the community from becoming an organized crime syndicate. The Rastas neither buy nor sell their labor power for a profit. In addition, the love of playfulness long into the night and the enjoyment of leisure by the male Rastas militate against any mobilization of labor power to stake out sites that are free of police surveillance, grow more herb, and develop a system of networks that could tie them into the international drug trade. All of these activities are rational calculations to accumulate profits, and as such they are unlikely behavior patterns among Lion, Nigel, their friends, and the Rastas at the beach.

In spite of their low economic productivity, the Rastas do not evince the despair of the Jamaican poor, manifest in the break up of family ties and a rampant alcoholism through addiction to rum. Were one to venture into Kingston's ghettos or an environ near Kingston called "Sufferah's Heights," for instance, it becomes clear that poverty has individualized and polarized the community to such an extent that terror controls one's life. The people fear one another, and crippling to all is the violence of theft, rape and witchcraft. Furthermore, their acquiescence to the will of God who has mysteriously placed them there makes alternatives impossible. Rastas also live there, but they have appraised the situation differently. Indeed, in the midst of poverty, one Rasta sustains himself and his family by crafting handbags and sandals. His nickname is Shocker because, in an example of Rasta ingenuity, his is the only family with electricity on those "Sufferah's Heights." Shocker says that his Rasta beliefs direct him toward this world rather than toward a better life in a world to come. Rastas like Shocker develop all the resources at their disposal. At the beach, there is fishing and cultivation of land; on the streets, there is hustling.

In the opinion of the Christian Jamaican, Rastas like Nigel and the others are atheists. They do not attend an established church. They disdain belief in the spirit world and show contempt for those who invite spirit possession and trance. The Rastas, however, view their impiety in a positive light. They put it that they will not board the slave ship of religion again. Their language about Jah Rastafari is intended to empower themselves rather than a supernatural other. For these Rastas and others like them, no divinity exists beyond time and space. That much is certain. The Rastas are practical and cunning, and their belief in Jah Rastafari is part of this worldly wisdom.

Ganja

Ever since estate wage labor took hold in Jamaica at the turn of this century, ganja has been part of the lower working-class culture. This began with the importation of ganja and cheap laborers from India. Thenceforth, ganja smoking received an indirect nod of approval from the upper classes because they realized that ganja guaranteed that the workers would be productive. Ganja acted as a stimulant and incentive to work. The pleasures of ganja were enough to compensate the laborer for a toilsome day's labor in the fields. Ganja was shared at convivial gatherings, and these sustained the workingmen. Ganja was a legitimate aspect of working-class life among the black population. The customs surrounding its use made it into a rite of passage for working-class life in the fields. The first taking of the spliff was a sign that a youth was ready to start his life's work in the cane fields.

The Rastas, however, deconstruct the ordinary socialization process around ganja. They reverse the meanings of the use of ganja which have reinforced the norms of working class culture. Dread, Nigel, and Lion use ganja in order to find illumination and insight into the wretched conditions of the black man and woman caught up in the service of Babylon. Ganja does not lighten the burden of an oppressive day's work because their labor is self-serving. Their economic activities are not part of the process of buying and selling labor power for profit but are filled with emancipatory possibilities.

Aided by ganja, their reasoning moves Rasta participants to chant doom on Babylon and affirm the equality of all people. During their reasoning session, they may denounce the hypocrisy of government and church because they have manipulated their authority to enslave people. The Rastas' language and demeanor no longer share much with the social discourse of the society around them, and their gatherings are spontaneous and communal rather than routinized and focused on the individual. Indeed, when a Rasta initiate brings the baggage of status and prestige into the group, he is challenged by a swirling chorus of accusations, innuendo, fierce gestures and hostile shouting. The Rastas reject the notion of social inequality which is taken for granted in the larger society. Their journey into illumination upsets the structures or orderliness, propriety and respectability demanded by Jamaican society. "Church and state, law and society and parliamentary democracy, you gone!" Aware of this, the Christian fundamentalists are quick to label the Rastas as devil worshippers. Nevertheless, what they perceive as profanation is, in the eyes of the Rastas, both destructive and creative. Their rage against established order is meant to restore it to an equilibrium.

Toward Accommodation

Not all Rastas nurture the spontaneity and freedom that Lion, Nigel and the others enjoy. At quite a social distance from them are Lloyd and Gordon. For them, the social mores of middle-class Jamaican society are not particularly oppressive. The tenets of Rastafari provide them with another opportunity for differentiating themselves from their neighbors.

Lloyd and Gordon do not disrupt the patterns of middle class life at Pierport. They do not usurp the role of women in the household and their authority over children, as does Dread at the beach, for example. Their wives are not subservient to them in every instance—they command the respect of the community because they maintain impeccable households, attend the local church and raise their children properly. They emphasize the value of the nuclear family rather than the extended family of the Rastas. The smoking of marijuana is a private affair among the men, and the activity does not compromise the moral standards of the community. There are no ceremonies surrounding its use, no panegyric about its illuminative potential. Instead the herb is praised for its sweetness, a position quite acceptable to the dominant classes who indulge in it from time to time as a means of pleasure and a respite from daily stress. Lloyd and Gordon's economic activities are dependent on the capitalist marketplace and not on a material base of local self-sufficiency. All of the above indicate an accommodating tendency among these Rastas, who manipulate the tenets of

Rastafari so that they serve their own interests as middle-class Jamaican males.

To better understand how the syncretism represented by the lives of Lloyd and Gordon is possible, it is useful to consider for a moment how the economic development of a nation can affect the cultural values of its people. Some social critics have argued that advanced capitalist societies tend to subordinate cultural identities to economic interests. In advanced capitalist nations such as the United States, for example, cultural values lost their distinctive significance and are subsumed by various economic strategies such as union contracts, litigations and tax payments, which make people's lives susceptible to unintentional corruption. Cultural values become privatized and thrive on supposedly rational norms like competition and merit. In contrast, the values that surround the productivity of Nigel, Lion and Dread are self-determined and personal, rooted in kinship, blackness, Haile Selassie and other elements of Rasta belief. These values limit rather than increase the productive potential of the Rastas. They are premodern values which Rastas use as a means of differentiating themselves; they are values which create a social enclave for the Rastas and they do not serve the interests of capital accumulation and cannibalize premodern values.

Not every aspect of Jamaican life has been subjected to transformation into a commodity for the sake of profit. For instance, even in middle-class Pierport, membership in a church and personal norms such as respectability rather than consumption still determine social status. At this point in Jamaica, modern categories of class differentiation such as consumption are still struggling for control. While the dominant political parties proceed on the assumption that the building blocks of Jamaican society are an individual's ability to allocate resources in the competitive marketplace, premodern values still command the social consciousness of Jamaican society. These values still retain their prominence in a social ranking system that is not yet economically determined; systems of kinship, ranking and family life are, as yet, still influenced by local traditional phenomena.

Jamaica is a nation, then, where class consciousness is not fully developed along economic lines. While the people of Pierport do differentiate themselves from their neighbors, these distinctions are not fully dependent on economic values. Among the Rastas in Pierport, the basis for differentiation lies in cultural values such as masculinity and male bonding, tenets of Rastafari that bolster the self-assertion of the middle-class Jamaican male as well. Furthermore, since the political parties have been using the symbols of

Rastafari since 1970, a Jamaican male can easily manipulate his way into the patronage system through his belief in Rastafari.

In the past decade, Jamaica has been vying for a stronger foothold in the capitalist market. It is striving for an advanced economy. These aspirations must be accepted by the Jamaican mainstream if this policy is to succeed. Since Rastafari had its origins as an authentic Jamaican tradition, it could be co-opted by the Jamaican middle class and elite to serve their own political and economic goals. The establishment of a class society in Jamaica would then be perceived as a natural flow from the past. By appropriating some of the values of Rastafari, the middle class could give itself a firmer foothold in Jamaica's economic development. The bourgeoisie could use Rastafari to show that economic stratification is the natural historical outcome of Jamaican history. The hierarchies of capitalism in Jamaica could be presented as the logical sequence to earlier communitarian divisions in society.

As we shall see, however, the Rastafarian movement is not a committed partner in this co-optation and manipulation of its symbols and beliefs.

The Rastafari and the
Jamaican State

Jamaican society responds with great ambivalence toward the Rastafari. For instance, among the parishioners at the Catholic Church in Kingston and entrepreneurs in that city are some who admire the Rastafari verve. However, their admiration would never lead them to join with the Rastafari or allow their children to do so. This attitude reflects the ambivalence that permeates a society going through political and economic changes. The halting acceptance granted the Rastafari mirrors the economic transformations that are creating a watershed in Jamaican history.

Rational and Subsistence Economies

Social scientists have argued that Jamaica is poised on a dilemma between a mode of production based on capitalist enterprise and one dependent on the subsistence economies of a localized peasantry. Capitalism is understood here as a drive to amass wealth and power by an appropriation of resources from a labor force stratified by class interests. Here bureaucratization prevails, and commodification and consumption reign supreme. The peasantry, however, is a labor force not so beholden to wage labor; peasants are self-sufficient on their land. Reciprocity and redistribution bind their social relationships. The capitalist argues that this mode of production is not geared toward the rational accumulation of wealth

65

and power. There is truth in this. Other areas of concern such as religion, respectability, storytelling, and so on command the peasantry's interest. The realm of rational economics takes a secondary role in peasant life and is subservient to other cultural interests. In supplanting the peasantry, the bureaucratization of capitalist production is based on the belief that "with increasing intellectualization and rationalization all things can be controlled by means of calculation." In short, economic interests prevail over all others and cannibalize all other values.

To be sure, the domination of capitalism has not yet been fully realized in Jamaica, whose pluralistic society holds more interests than the calculatingly economic ones. The varying interests of Jamaicans, resistant to economic rationality, unsettle the liberal bourgeoisie electoral campaigns. The result is often a dramatic confrontation expressed in party violence when Jamaicans must choose between the socialism of the PNP and the capitalist adventurism of the JLP. Political parties touting economic development of the state on the part of the right or the left do not capture the imagination of the people. Commitment to the state is weak. The average Jamaican is more concerned with resolution of feuds, redress or grievances against others, and revenge, than the rational politics of either party. What emerges in political violence are the residues of long-standing grievances among families and social groups rather than claims based on the interests of the bourgeoisie. Thus, a clearly defined national interest in a market economy and the development of the state has so far eluded Jamaican society.

Jamaican society exemplifies a pluralistic culture occupied with many interests other than a monolithic one based on the bureaucratization of economic development. The ethos of Rastafari develops within the pluralism of Jamaican society and the struggles that modernization implies, i.e. bourgeois versus peasant. Many Jamaicans sympathize with the brothers and sisters of Rastafari because they express a traditional cultural identity, rooted in the affirmation of black pride and resistance to racial subordination. Nevertheless, the same Jamaicans realize that the commitment to Rastafari may not be a particularly rational way to amass wealth and power. Hence, the middle class vacillates in its attitudes toward Rastafari. The social goals of the middle class look toward economic development and bureaucratization while the Rasta brothers and sisters are not so inclined.

Proselytizing efforts on the rewards of modernization are penetrating Jamaican society with an increasing vigor, and the working-class ethic continues to compete for a position of ascendancy in Jamaican society. The media, for one, trumpet the success stories of business and governmental projects. The tourist industry, agricultural schemes, civil service positions, and a burgeoning insurance industry are persuasive propaganda in the hands of those calling for a modern, bureaucratized society in Jamaica. The civil servant and the factory worker are the ideal. Progress is the watchword. The educational system, the media and the politicians convey the message of a working class ethic to the citizenry. The Jamaican past, rooted as it was in a free peasantry even though subject to British imperialism, is seen as an anachronism embraced only by the "uneducated country boys."

Rastafari and the State

Since the 1930s Jamaican society has been wrestling with the problem of how to transform the moral basis of its peasantry into a working class without the use of force that threatened the stability of the labor class in 1938. A modern state attempting to impose itself on a resistant peasantry must arraign itself with a panoply of

Rastas reject the modernization of Jamaica where the civil servant and the factory worker are the ideal. (United Nations)

symbols to make itself credible. Jamaican society is moving toward modernization and bureaucratization through this social process, which seems endemic to the development of western states. That is, in order to strengthen its power base, the state welcomes the embodiment of folk symbols in its national identity.

Jamaican folk symbols in the persons of Sam Sharpe, Paul Bogle and Marcus Garvey have already become symbols for the state. During patriotic celebrations on Independence Day, images of the national heroes are paraded before the public at the national stadium in Kingston. Meanwhile, raggae musicians, espousing the sentiments of Rastafari, sing out the path to freedom and African identity. All of this appears under the auspices of the Jamaican bureaucracy personalized in its governmental officials and representatives of the church and business. The national celebration is a drama legitimizing the modern state. Indeed, any modern state must justify itself through a symbolic life that goes beyond merely materialistic goals. Rastafari is a symbol available to the modern Jamaican state and accessible to all.

Rastafari holds a wealth of memories that resound with themes of justice: its closeness to the land, its bias toward African identity, and its call to black awareness. Its discourse can serve as a part of the symbolism from which the state can draw its strength and demonstrate its rootedness in the historical past. Thus, traditional values will appear to be the grounding of the modern state. Yet the appropriation of these values actually masks the exploitations in class relations. State bureaucrats awaken the memories of folk traditions in a self-serving expression of national pageantry. The state then transforms the ethos of Rastafari into an instrument that will sustain a working-class culture in Jamaica. Black pride is linked to the national destiny of economic progress. Furthermore, the themes of freedom from oppression and slavery, familiar enough to the Rastafari, become fused with a working-class ethic, which the modern bourgeois state then hails as emancipatory and progressive.

Of course, this is ironic. What was initially a rejection of modernity is turning into a symbolic base for its acceptance. It seems outrageous to suggest that the working-class culture can appropriate the symbols of Rastafari, a way of life that has been so militantly opposed to the "boss man." Yet, this is indeed becoming the case. The resistance that the Rasta movement had demonstrated against modernization in the 1930s and 1940s has diminished. Certainly the electoral campaigns of the 1970s indicated this. That was a time when Rastafari gained a place in the national consciousness through the efforts of Michael Manley, the PNP candidate for Prime Minister.

Rastas and the Working Class

The independence of Jamaica in 1962, the expanding capitalist economy and the electoral campaign of the 1970s that favored Rastafari symbolism, have helped to meld that symbolism with the working class. Especially persuasive in this transformation has been the emergence of a new class, whose members were highly sympathetic to the ways of Rastafari. The brown population, together with some blacks, has taken on the role of the managerial class for international capitalists, accepting the hegemony of a working-class life marked by competitiveness, profit and individualism. Now all believe that they can be prosperous. Black Jamaicans own and operate stores in fashionable shopping malls in Kingston whose businesses sometimes deal in the commodities of the successful reggae music industry. Rasta can mean successful business!

The domination of capitalist ideology has advanced since the 1930s, and the ways of production embedded in a peasant way of life are on the wane. Through modernization, the Rastafari symbols lose their material base in the peasantry and become susceptible to capitalist or socialist interests. For instance, by 1977, Archibald Dunkley, an early leader in the Rasta movement, announced through a Rastafari publication entitled *The Ethiopian World* the fellowship between the movement and modernity. He wrote: "Outside of Marcus Garvey the only individual who has helped the people is our present Prime Minister, Michael Manley. . . . We find Michael has come to do the will of God for the Rastafarians."

Nevertheless, some Rastafari resent this co-optation. In a letter to the *Daily Gleaner*, Ras Mikeman underlined the importance of the Rastafari resistance to wage labor and modernism. He emphasized that the elders in the movement should instruct the young initiates to avoid participation in the politics of the Jamaican state. If the community were involved in the political and economic goals of the state, Mikeman argued, this would draw the Rastafari into the corruptions of the body politic. Such an alliance with the powers of the state would cause them to lose their African identity and their desire to repatriate to Africa. Mikeman admonished the Rasta brothers and sisters to maintain their communal ties and remain aloof from the trickery of the Jamaican state. Mikeman's suggestions are established practices among many contemporary

Rasta and non-Rasta Jamaicans earn a livelihood playing reggae music for tourists. (Joan Gregg)

Rastafari, and not all have accommodated themselves to the goals of the state. Their communes on the beaches of southern Jamaica and their foundation at Bull Bay are poignant reminders that the Rastafari still have the cultural wisdom to resist the liberal encroachments of the modern state.

The Rastafarian movement, no matter how much the state tries to co-opt its symbolism, remains grounded in the peasant way of Jamaican life. The Rastas maintain a stock of symbols around Haile Selassie, repatriation, marijuana and language that revitalizes the threatened culture of a disbanded peasantry. Their tradition of self-sustaining occupations such as fishing, handicrafts and general hustling are enterprises based on the productivity of extended, familial networks. This lifestyle mirrors that of the peasantry and cannot sustain the total organization of a labor force under the discipline of the market economy. Nevertheless, like Jamaican society, the Rastafarian movement harbors within itself a dialectical tension: the one pole planted in the self-sustaining materialistic and symbolic world of the peasantry and the other sympathetic with the interests of the modern bourgeoisie.

Ambivalence

In spite of the co-optation of the movement and the resistance of some Rastafari to the state, there can be no definitive answer on how they are perceived in Jamaican society. Each Jamaican grants the Rastafari a place in society based on what social position he or she inhabits, viewing the Rastas from a particular "set of cultural ideas and social institutions." The poor, the brown middle class and the creole whites each address the Rastafari according to their own social interests. Variation is the norm. This was evident on the occasion of the funeral of the raggae musician Bob Marley, when Prime Minister Edward Seaga presided at what appeared to be a state funeral, yet many in the middle class took exception to this display of public sentiment for so prominent a Rastafari. The pluralistic nature of the Jamaican state inhibits a dominant social or legal characterization of the Rastafari. In other words, conflicting opinions about the Rastafari in Jamaican society are products of its pluralism.

Jamaica has not even created a social niche for the Rastafari that can be compared with the accommodation that the United States has etched out for such groups as the Amish and the Native American Church. Our state allowed the Amish to pursue their educational policies for their young and, to a lesser extent, allowed the Native Americans the use of the hallucinogenic plant Peyote in their religious services. Our legal process was able to accommodate such dissenting groups without compromising the common good or commonwealth. It appears that Jamaican society enjoys no such sense of common good among its citizenry.

The advanced capitalist nations of England and the United States have developed a self-serving view of the Rasta movement which reduces it to a one-sided psychological or political analysis. From the psychological point of view, the worth of Rastafari is in the option it provides individuals who are in search of a personal identity amidst the depersonalization of advanced capitalism. The tenets of Rastafari, it is argued, may project a more positive self-image than the beliefs of Christianity, the values of parents or the goals of educational institutions. Rastafari is but a stepping stone to maturity. One author, for example, wrote about the experience of his son who embraced Rastafari, but by eighteen years of age had abandoned that posture and taken up a career in the social sciences. If not a psychological reduction, Rastafari may receive a political gloss. Here the brothers and sisters are viewed as political activists whose goals are to overcome racism and poverty in the marketplace.

Whether political or psychological, these are ethnocentric viewpoints which cannot generate a cultural understanding of Rastafari. They do not really capture the cultural resistance of Rastafari to modernism. Instead, the political or psychological interpretations of the movement recast it along the lines that the Eurocentric person can appreciate. Advanced capitalism redefines the movement so that it suffers a trivialization that would be unlikely in Jamaican society. Cultural values are at the source of the difference.

Unlike the United States or England, Jamaican society glories in its identity as the very quintessence of the black pride that permeates the Rastafarian ethos. England and the United States may glory in the capitalist revolutions that transformed their states into capitalistic, middle class societies, but among the Jamaican people, the revolution has been a rejection of its racially stratified past. Jamaican society no longer labels blackness as a source of alienation. The struggles of the Jamaican people over slavery and racism are culturally significant for many. In contrast, capitalism is paramount for the majority of the people in England and the United States. Therein lies the difference.

Yet this should not imply that the Rastafari enjoy the unequivocal allegiance of everyone in Jamaican society. There is ambivalence, as my conversations with a Jamaican police official, reported in the next chapter, reveal. This police officer's perspective on the Rasta is much more complex than the psychological or political reductionism found in capitalist nations. While, in the final analysis he is uncertain about where the Rastas fit into Jamaican society, he is capable of understanding the movement on a level beyond that of his peers in England or the United States.

7

The Deputy Inspector and
the Rastas

Deputy Inspector Dunston, a pseudonym, reflects the ambivalence of Jamaican society toward the Rastas. Because the Jamaican legal code has not yet found an accommodating niche for the Rastas, Dunston relies for the most part on his own discretionary powers when dealing with Rastas.

In the absence of a legal language about Rastas, Dunston has not made up his mind whether the Rastas are troublemakers or respectable citizens. His articulation is halting and contradictory in this matter. What he does have, however, is a wealth of experience that puts his understanding and discussion of the Rastas into a highly particularistic context. He resorts, in other words, to local knowledge and communal norms of respectability rather than referring to legal statutes. Within this personal, informal context, he views the Rastas as part of his official responsibility. Interestingly, whereas in the more advanced industrialized societies of the West there is a heavy reliance on formal statutes and norms that are universally applicable throughout society, Jamaicans such as Deputy Inspector Dunston seem to prefer an *ad hoc* system of justice in dealing with Rastas and others. Marijuana is a relevant issue here.

Dunston supervises the regulation of the marijuana trade so that its traffic is restrained. Toward that end his office is charged with the task of seizing marijuana crops from hidden fields in the interior that his informants and patrols have discovered. Teams then destroy the ganja in huge bonfires along deserted beachfronts of southern Jamaica. Sometimes pressures mount on the inspector to be more effective. These pressures come from the United States, which has threatened to reduce financial aid if the Jamaican authorities do not make more progress in stifling the ganja trade. One might surmise that the involvement of the Rastas in ganja would cause them to be the inspector's primary concern. However, this does not turn out to be the case. No evidence has linked them to the international ganja trade.

Inquiries about the relationship between Rastas and the police do not particularly disturb Dunston, at least at the beginning of the discussion. The international drug business, he believes, is under the control of organized crime from whose influence he excludes the Rastas. The Rastas present no particular problem for the efficient realization of his duties which involve the curtailment of the drug traffic.

Rastas and the Courts

Magistrates, too, are unwilling to affix the label of organized crime to Rastafarian activities. From the late 1960s onward, records from the Court of Appeals for Criminal Offenses do not disclose any cases in which a Rasta was interrogated for an alleged connection to an international drug ring. This has been the state of affairs even when a Rasta was apprehended under circumstances that pointed to a heavy involvement in the sale of ganja. In one court hearing in 1965, for example, it was argued that a Rasta convicted in the parish of St. Catherine for unlawful possession of money could not have acquired such a large sum from wages because he was known to be unemployed. This strongly implied that the money was ganja related. Yet, while the acquisition of wealth by the Rasta group might have been questioned, and their violations of the market economy might have been explored in this case, this did not happen and the issue of organized crime was never raised.

The Rastas clash with the law only when their cultivation of marijuana attracts public attention. "Why bother the small men in the ganja traffic?" Deputy Inspector Dunston asks. Incidents that involve the theft of their crops, for instance, might very well lead to violence which will distress the neighborhood and bring in the police. Ordinarily problems of this nature are rare, and the Rastas maintain a respectable profile in the community by fulfilling their duties as fathers or providers for their families. Generosity, a willingness to share, and an allegiance to the welfare of the local community are traits that shield the Rastas' unlawful dealings in marijuana from the interference of the law. The local knowledge of events is determining. The application of a universalistic legal statute is inappropriate when dealing with the Rastas.

Dunston sums it up:

"Our policy is not to hunt down a Rastaman. If a Rasta smokes in private, that means he is showing respect for the law. It is desirable that he smoke at home or in hiding so that the law may not be disrespected."

Indeed, the use of marijuana among the Rastas is such a known and socially accepted fact that there are no recorded cases in which lawyers have argued for a more lenient treatment for Rastas because of their religious use of it. Dunston notices that magistrates tend to be more lenient with a Jamaican Rasta on charges involving violations of the Dangerous Drugs Act. However, the courts are not so full of largess for the foreign offender.

Attitudes toward Rastas have changed. Dunston remembers that during the 1950s the Rastas were considered deviants by police, who routinely harassed them. Then the police would question them on the streets at the slightest provocation and shear their locks to humiliate them. Since the 1980s, however, the situation has been different. Dunston proudly asserts that the Rastas are now part of Jamaican culture. When asked about any educational programs regarding the Rastas that the police are required to take, he replied that there is no reason for this, so the police do not receive any special training in this area. The Rastas are not considered a public menace, and Dunston claims there is no reason for the police to be trained about their own culture, implying that the Rastas are part of that culture. Here, I believe, we have a clear demonstration of how Dunston's reliance on local knowledge and experience, rather than any universalistic or "scientific" approach to the Rastas, aids his understanding. This contrasts markedly with the approach in the United States, where police in large metropolitan areas ordinarily get specific instruction on the "Rasta menace."

Dunston praises the Jamaican police, who create lines of communication between themselves and the Rastas. The fewer tensions there are between the police and the Rastas, the better, because the Rastas can aid the police in efficiently executing their duties. In Jamaica there is no pressure exerted by the police on the Rastas to desist from selling marijuana. Hardly ever do the police raid Rastafarian communities in search of the illegal drug. The Jamaican police are not charged with the task of bringing the Rastas into conformity with the law with the intensity that drives the British police. The Jamaican type of cooperative situation is a contrast to that in Birmingham, England, for instance, where, since the mid-1970s, the Rastas have been co-opted to police their own communities.

Dunston's Ambivalence

The positive attitudes Deputy Inspector Dunston holds toward the Rastas are balanced by his misgivings and uncertainties about the movement. Dunston is a representative of the working-class ethic. The Rastas re-creation of the image of a self-sustaining peasantry antithetical to the necessity of wage labor is undoubtedly the basis of Dunston's ambivalence toward them. Dunston knows about the Rasta acquisition of wealth through nonorthodox means that circumvent the labor market. He belongs to that social milieu which, with its increasing bureaucratization, professionalism, urbanization and literacy, has very little tolerance for the deviant and marginal ways in which the Rasta earn their livelihoods. The spontaneous and noncontractual way through which the Rasta commune at Bull Bay supports itself as a squatter on the land, for example, is hardly the normal choice for the Jamaican, like Dunston, who is interested in class mobility and worker protection. And while some Jamaicans may even understand that the business of marijuana is a necessary correlate to a weak economy, they would hardly regard that business as an enterprise which safeguards workers' contracts and wages. In truth, Dunston begrudges the Rastas the wealth they have amassed through their handiworks, hustling and ganja. These enterprises are all too cunning for the average workers whose lives are determined by the factory clock.

In particular Dunston disdains the reggae musicians who congregate on the grounds of the estate of the late Bob Marley, now a monument to reggae music. "They live like higher caste English people." His reference to caste is revealing because a Jamaican tends to identify the concept of caste with white elitism, privilege and snobbery, which oppose both the working-class ethic and the principles of the liberal, democratic state.

"How then," he adds, "can the Rastas tell us they are oppressed when they live the ways of the elite?"

Dunston's position is not simply an argument bemoaning class differences, although economic stratification plays its part in Jamaican society. His is much more of a disagreement based on a cultural perspective. The Rastas extol blackness, sacralize things African and yearn for repatriation to Africa. These are symbolic values which negate the secular approach to the acquisition of wealth, a cherished value among the working class. Indeed, the Rastas do not separate the realm of religion from that of the political-economic sphere, as the bourgeois world tends to do. They are different, and in registering this difference, Dunston's approach reflects the cultural pluralism of a society that has not yet been able to accommodate the differences with the goal of economic expansionism.

Thus, Dunston can be ambivalent about his position on marijuana, not from the perspective of the legal market, for he understands the need to supplement one's income in a depressed economy, but from a cultural viewpoint. He expresses a clear distaste for the Rastas' selling of ganja when they claim it is a sacrament. Their success in this business venture causes him to question but not discredit their claims that ganja is used for religious purposes. "How can a man make money by selling sacraments?" Again, here he implies a preference for the separation of religious goals from economic ones, a typically bourgeois position that effectively maintains an equilibrium in advanced industrial states.

Dunston addresses the question of Rasta marijuana use through his own working-class ethic. Marijuana, he believes, destroys the vitality and motivation of the youth to work. But although he offers some observations on the baneful effects of marijuana, he nevertheless reserves a special aside for the case of the Rastas. This hedging on the question confirms the pluralistic nature of Jamaican society, which makes a distinction between the middle class and the Rastas.

This same society has also attempted to wear down its pluralism by co-opting the Rastas into the working-class ethic. The situation is complex, and Dunston's remarks highlight one aspect of that complexity.

When questioned about studies that show that ganja is not a dangerous drug, Dunston retorts: "It is not safe to smoke ganja. Ganja has a bad effect on youth. Youths are walking the streets of Kingston, naked and crazy, because of chillum (pipe) smoking. There is no such thing as the controlled use of ganja. I do not agree with those studies on ganja. Ganja makes people stupid. At least rum wears away. Ganja stays in the system. It accumulates in the body. Ganja causes people to commit serious crime because of its influence on the mind. It does not let the person fulfill his duties to society."

In spite of these misgivings about marijuana, however, there is a cultural nuance to his discussion that contradicts his attempt to find a universal solution to this issue. Despite his negative views about the drug in general, Dunston has observed that it has a therapeutic effect on Rastas, observations derived from his experiences in the Kingston ghetto.

"After all," he notes, "seldom are the poor Rastas as ill as their neighbors who do not use ganja to the extent that the Rastas do. They seem protected."

Even his experiences with Rastas who are incarcerated lead him to affirm some beneficial effects of ganja.

"Generally the others in prison are more violent. The Rastas have a calmer attitude when arrested. They are much calmer."

"Then," I said, "you have a live and let live attitude toward Rastafari."

"Yes," he answered and laughed.

Rastas and Legal Status

The plural nature of Jamaican society has traditionally been exempt from the incursion of the law and the intervention of the state. The protection or suppression of social differences have been left to the discretion of the local communities. In spite of trends that show the necessity for a state to incorporate its varied cultural groups within a single national framework, the responses of Jamaican society to the Rastas is permissive of their cultural differences. People do not psychologize them, nor reduce them to economic considerations alone, paradigms of the more advanced capitalist societies whose legal codes take a rational approach to divergent cultural groups. Deputy Inspector Dunston's testimony indicates how the average working-class Jamaican perceives the Rastas: they are seen as another culture with values and norms of their own. At the same time, the socialistic government is still attempting to incorporate certain Rasta elements into its own economic and political structure. Thus we see reflected in the tension between the Rastas and the Jamaican state the give-and-take nature of a pluralistic society.

Jamaica has not yet crossed that threshold of development whereby the legal system can precisely identify the appropriate place for subcultural groups, as happens in the United States. Instead of legal precedent and judgments, Jamaican magistrates and police follow the norms of respectability in the community, a type of local knowledge rather than statutory law. Dunston operates on this principle. For the most part, he relies on his own discretionary powers to guide him in rendering the Rastas their just due.

The inspector's method of dealing with the Rastas derives from common law and legal irrationality, procedures documented by the jurist Benjamin Cardozo and the social scientist Max Weber. Cardozo explained that the use of common law meant that custom, rather than the strict application of legal statutes, decided a case. In this light, the Rastas' smoking of marijuana is viewed as part of their customary behavior rather than as a flagrant violation of the Dangerous Drugs Act. This perception of their behavior as cultural rather than criminal works well for them in the courts, in contrast to the view held of the foreigner caught dealing in the drug.

This Jamaican approach to justice is what Max Weber has called legal irrationality. For in Jamaica, we have an application of case-by-case decisions made by judges in accordance with the facts of each specific case. The judicial outcome is based primarily on ethical, political and social considerations, not formal rules encoded in law. In Jamaica, the procedures of both common law and legal irrationality create legal facts through the consent of the local community. It is this consent, and not the dictates of some over-seeing legislative body, which determines what does and does not count. This helps explain why the Jamaican police do not raid the commune at Bull Bay, the fishing villages along the coast or the many Rasta "mansions" throughout the city of Kingston for drug busts. Of course, the application of the process of legal irrationality will not always be favorable to the Rastas. In the 1970s and 1980s, the social climate of Jamaica was more favorable to the group than it had been in the past when police raided their commune at the Pinnacle.

Divided Loyalties

A commonwealth such as that enjoyed by the United States does not yet exist in Jamaica. Issues such as ethnicity, race, respect-ability and level of education rather than economic interests alone still command the attention of the Jamaican people. This attests to the plural nature of Jamaican society, many of whose people owe allegiance both to the work ethic inculcated by international capitalism and the traditions of the local community. Sustained by this plural context, the Rastas can still flourish as a subculture.

The modern Jamaican state, however, if it wishes to be a commonwealth of bourgeois interests, must above all else legitimate itself and win the consent of its citizens. The legitimacy of the market economy and expansionism must be assured. One way of accomplishing this is to create the impression that the modern state is the outgrowth of the traditional struggles against slavery, colonialism and racism. Toward this end, the symbols of Rastafari can be an appropriate vehicle, for they have emerged from a communal consciousness of oppression. Through the appropriation of the Rastafarian symbols, then, the market economy can be linked to the struggles of the slaves, the assertion of black identity, the natural goodness of the Jamaican soil, and the African roots of the black Jamaican. In this manner, the movement appears to be aligned with the national state and loses its identity as a subcultural movement in a pluralistic setting. There is evidence for this appropriation of the movement's symbols by the state.

In the 1980s throughout the metropolitan centers of Jamaica, Rastas can be seen managing stores that distribute reggae music and running restaurants that serve ital foods to the influx of tourists as well as Jamaicans. Other Rastas live in middle-class housing projects. These Rastas may still smoke the herb, reason about Haile Selassie, long for repatriation to Africa and bemoan the evils of Babylon. Now, however, these reasonings take place on their verandas overlooking the Kingston harbor while their wives serve fruit drinks to their guests. This suggests that some in Jamaican middle-class society can succeed in transforming at least some symbols of the Rastafarian movement into their own more mainstream ideology.

Whether capitalist relations will ultimately dominate in Jamaica is uncertain. The contradictions between a capitalist mode of production and a mode of production independent of world capitalism lie at the basis of the struggles of the Jamaican people. The violence at national elections, when Jamaicans are asked to choose between the socialist People's National Party and the capitalist Jamaica Labour Party bears testimony to this. The ethos of Rastafari impales itself on the horns of this dilemma. It can cooperate with the economic and political system of the developing state by involving its members, such as reggae musicians, in contracts and unions, or, it can motivate its members to acquire wealth through unorthodox means that threaten the stability of the labor market. Both options are familiar to Jamaicans, and both seem to have acquired social respectability in this contradictory society.

Urban Rastas, U.S.A.

The United States is home for a large number of West Indians, especially Jamaicans. They have set down roots in urban neighborhoods seeking the economic security broadcast so triumphantly by those who manage the interest of international capitalism in the Caribbean. Sometimes this promise delivers. My focus in this chapter is on one Jamaican neighborhood that thrives in an American metropolis. Here brisk businesses flourish. The establishments feature ethnic foods, entertainment and accents. Legitimate businesses reflect the success of capitalist investment, but they are only one facet of the neighborhood. Sprinkled here and there are stores from which Rastas pursue their way of life, often to the chagrin of their more acculturated neighbors.

The Rasta shops feature various and sundry goods. Some Rasta merchants manufacture and distribute T-shirts stenciled with designs of the Lion of Judah and other Rastafarian symbols. Others are skilled tailors who craft fine leather clothing. Whatever is distinctive about their style of life, if it lends itself to aesthetic expression, it is likely to find its outlet in these stores. As an adjunct to their legitimate enterprises, most of these Rasta businesses engage in the sale of marijuana.

Ras, Rabu, Ashi and Baba are Rastas from Jamaica who now live quite prosperously in this metropolitan area. Their life adventures interconnect and read like tales from Trickster literature. Indeed, their interaction with the rest of the community is a dramatic scenario that always contains a moral lesson of one kind or another.

Viewed in contention with the police, their dramas epitomize the Rasta as Anancy, that divine-human trickster originating in African folklore and preserved in the tales of the Jamaican peasantry. Trickster prevails despite all the odds, and so do the Rastas.

The Rastas try to maintain a respectable appearance as the guardians of the peace and examples of justice and the shared life. The Rastas work, care for their children and look out for each other's welfare with as much vigilance as any other West Indian group in the neighborhood. Their "smoke shops" may be the dispensaries for marijuana, but they are also places of conviviality where neighborhood males, fully cognizant of Rastafarian proclivities but not Rastas themselves, may relax, converse and form friendships. The shops nurture networks of mutual support. Here one can spend hours in leisure, just chatting, playing dominoes and watching television shows.

The Rastas forge their identity with a sense of radical distinctiveness in a society that tolerates differences only when the law permits it. From this cultural niche arises their conflict with the law, more poignant than in the Jamaica they left, which has all the ingredients of a dramatic liturgy.

In the final analysis, these Rastas are neither the friends of the police nor the compatriots of their Jamaican neighbors. Their connection to the marijuana trade, their aggressive attitudes and general hostility toward authority, combined with a sensitivity and respect for their unassuming fellow human beings, make them unique in this middle-class Caribbean neighborhood. With the exception of Prince, who publishes his views, all these Rasta prefer a low profile in the community and do not participate in community politics. All share a common bond, encourage one another's self-sufficiency and find an identity in their communal marginality.

Ras

Ras is an entrepreneur and philosopher.

He manages a T-shirt business that employs only Rasta brothers and sisters. The store specializes in emblazoning T-shirts with Rasta sayings and images such as "One Love," "Black Heart," and the likenesses of Marcus Garvey and Haile Selassie. The enterprise is such a success that it exports its products to Jamaica where Rasta elders are pleased to receive gifts purchased from Ras's store.

Ras also writes and publishes pamphlets that expound the philosophical principles of Rastafari, which he thinks of as treatises. For instance, his "We Condemn the False Theory and Corruption of Modern Babylon" and "Ras Speaks to Rastafari" are essays that criticize modern society through a genre that glories in the use of shock phrases to emphasize the message. For example, Ras does not shrink from describing the social environment as the "fuckeries of the world in which Rastas find themselves" that is, in "the shitism of modern society." Like a prophet, Ras rails against modernism, condemns the police force, and scorns all developmental plans in the neighborhood.

Ras holds that the world will be destroyed because of its defilement of the family, love and peace. Pointing to the calamities that have befallen the city as signs of the times, he sees a warning from God in the power shortage that afflicted the city in the late 1970s.

"The city was struck with darkness when one of their transformers for their electrical generators was hit with a streak of lightning from the hands of Jah Almighty; but Babylon took no heed. Instead they chose to steal, kill, lie, mix with all manner of filth. And in all of this stinkiness that they, the Babylonians, created and live in, they choose to blame the black man, especially the Rastafari, for all their fuckeries."

Ras anticipates the destruction of modern society because it is based on false theory and corruption. Modern evils cannot be cured in any other way. The Rastas themselves will open the pit that waits for the punishment of Europe, America and the world. He depicts this final scene:

"They will be cast in and not one seed of the corrupted vine of Babylon shall escape this judgment, because there will be no place to run and there will be no place to hide."

Ras has approximated the day of this destruction.

"This verdict is and will be fully accomplished by the year Nineteen Ninety Nine. Not one day or a year later. Not one or any time longer."

Against this day of Armageddon, Ras urges the Rastas to store up food, clothing and to find a safe place for shelter because the signs indicate that the world will be destroyed by nuclear weapons.

With this view Ras finds little sense in a passion for work.

"What is the use of working so hard to accumulate more money than you need. This is crazy. Make money for the things you need, and don't work so hard."

Understandably, too, he doesn't subscribe to the philosophy and ideals of Martin Luther King, Jr. who, Ras believes "has sold out the black man for an American identity rather than an African one. He made the black man white."

Questions about law and order cause Ras to rejoin with his

observations on inequality, brutality and control. On the unequal distribution of justice Ras points out that other ethnic groups are permitted flexibility in matters of self rule. In a rhetorical aside to the police, he asks:

"When other sects or cults marched, and tore down your precinct to shreds, you did not seek to go to King Street and destroy their place of business. Then the Babylonian brute force never has any right to destroy, confiscate and captivate the merchants of the Rastafari family and their place of business. Don't you see you are a racist 'Hoik-hoink.'"

Ras's consciousness of police brutality is pitched. He exhorts:

"When the boys in blue, the force of oppression and brutality within the community, is on the rampage of madness, they don't give a damn as long as you are a Rastafari. To them you are their enemy, for in reality they seek no friendship, unless you are an informer against your people."

According to Ras, the police provoke the Rastas into deliberate and troublesome confrontation.

"The majority of the Babylonian brute force provokes I-n-I to create dangerous acts against them, for they walk and drive around with these ballistic arms."

He cites a conversation he overheard to support his belief that the police do brutalize the Rastas.

"I quote the Babylonian reaction. This is their actual words after they had gotten scared and panicky and ran for covers. 'Mother fucker, that ain't right, them mother fucking niggers are crazy, mother fucking crazy. They could get somebody killed around this fucking place. When I am going for a Rasta man, I have to carry a bullet proof vest, two nine millimeters, a rifle, a shotgun and a sledge hammer. I mean some heavy ammunition, man, because them Rastafarians is heavy, real heavy, man.' "

Ras interprets the conflict with the police in moralistic imagery. The battle has apocalyptic proportions and the victory is assured to the righteous Rastas. Ordinarily, religious language of an other worldly nature is odious to the Rastas who view it as a slave ship that will lead them into bondage. Accordingly, Ras's success with his business makes his symbolic language very much a part of material culture and not only a reference to transcendence. Ras's imagery empowers the Rastas to take up their lives as dramas and create a material kingdom of justice here on earth and in that way escape the Last Judgment. We might consider Ras's values bizarre in a city that professes a cosmopolitan and secular belief. Yet, Rabu, Ashi and Aba II play out the same drama of Ras's views and behavior.

The Smoke Shop

Across the street from Ras's T-shirt business is a Rasta smoke shop, so named by the police because one can purchase marijuana there. The huge floor space the shop occupies is partitioned in two in order to house a leather-crafting business on the one side and a distributive center for marijuana on the other. Few records are kept to mark any of the business transactions except small note pads which the store's managers use to enter the orders for caps, tams and pants. No ledgers record salaries, profits or expenses. Salaries are distributed at day's end from the proceeds of the day's intake. Of course, no taxes are collected.

A back room provides the working space for the processing of the marijuana. Here the Rastas unpack the large cellulose bags that contain the Jamaican or Colombian marijuana. Some of the ways the substance may have been smuggled into the country are

In American cities and Caribbean tourist centers Rastas earn a living by the manufacture and sale of T-shirts and leather goods. (Richard Kenefick)

bizarre. It may have entered the country concealed in the body of a woman who feigned pregnancy or even packed into the coffins of dead Jamaican-Americans whose bodies have been returned to the States for burial.

The marijuana is compressed into the bags. The first task in the process is to separate the lumps of herb into sizable portions for the nickel bags. The herb is stuffed into the nickel bags, manila envelopes two by three inches. Once the nickel bags have been filled with enough marijuana for about three spliffs or small cigarettes, they are sealed with tape and hurried through the backyards to other Rasta distributors.

To make a purchase at Rabu's shop, a customer enters the store and proceeds to the end of the room and an enclosed counter. There sits a Rasta, partially concealed behind a plexiglass partition. "One," "two," "three," or "five." The customer need say nothing else; the Rasta doles out the requested amount of nickel bags. The exchange takes place within seconds. Most of the customers, especially if they are white, visit the shop after dark in an effort to avoid detection by the police. They arrive by car and spend not more than several minutes parked in front of the store or double-parked on the street. As many as forty customers an hour seems to be the average.

The Rastas control their ganja trade. From beginning to end, the enterprise is in their hands. No outsiders or those connected with organized crime have infiltrated their business successfully. Indeed, they are ready to defend their interests in the trade against anyone, using bullets, if necessary.

Rabu is prominent among the group in the smoke shop. His controlling interest over the shop is tempered by the other Rastas who are also partial owners of the enterprise. Rabu is the most articulate of the group and is very cordial and amicable to visitors. In this he is unlike most Rastas, who usually probe unashamedly into a visitor's stance on religion, politics and society.

Rabu might sit with visitors in the store's entrance, offer them some herb, a wad of which he retrieves from his pocket, and inquire about the nature of their visit. Satisfied by the sincerity of my interest, he recalled how crime was a problem in the neighborhood before the Rastas moved there in the late 1970s. Their presence thwarted outsiders who plied heroin and cocaine on the streets. By forming networks among themselves, the Rastas seized control of the marijuana trade in the area and routed strangers from the neighborhood, sometimes using force. Since that time, the community has not been plagued with crime.

As I sit in the shop, patrol cars whiz around the corner and pause at the shop—the possibility of a drug bust weighs heavily, but Rabu shows no uneasiness.

"They believe that the Rastas are criminals, thieves, vagabonds, the scum of the earth. Cops have little use for our shops because we sell marijuana here."

He smiles when the patrol car drives on, puffs deeply from his spliff and remarks: "Rastas are self-reliant. They are independent. They don't fear evil." Gesturing to the patrol cars, he asserts: "Evil is a short time affair."

The chances of getting caught and imprisoned are high, but Rabu copes with the situation. "God is with us. That's why we take chances. Like selling herb. Yeah, we sell herb to make money. Why not? The system is corrupt. When the cops bust this place, they take everything. They just don't go after the herb. They take the leather, radios and personal property. And we are supposed to believe in the system?"

At this point, Rabu's commentary is interrupted by shouts, laughter and excited conversation in Jamaican patois which come from the back room. There five Rastas are enjoying a Bruce Lee movie while smoking ganja and working on their leather materials. Around the room in scattered piles are leather supplies of various colors and quality, the merchandise purchased from dealers who specialize in the procurement of shipments stolen from warehouses. In spite of the good time all are apparently enjoying, the work effort is intense and demands great skill. Leather is cut to fit the patterns and then carefully punctured with awls to hold the stitching. The finishing touches are applied with the aid of the sewing machine. The laughter subsides and Rabu continues:

"We are not Communists. That's what they said about us in Jamaica under Manley. We are not capitalists either. We just live. God will conquer evil in the end. Even jail doesn't frighten us. That's why we always fill our bellies with ital food. In case we have to go to jail, we'll at least go with bellies filled. They don't have ital food in jail."

Rabu drives a BMW automobile. Questions about his material prosperity and use of wealth stir up his reflections:

"Things are to be used. You get what you want, but that's all. We must be willing to share our things, drive people around and help people. Big egos get in the way."

Rabu's generosity surfaced later when he drove several Rastas into a fashionable section of the city to visit an expensive men's clothing shop. The proprietor greeted Rabu as he would a familiar customer. Rabu purchased a suit costing $800, in cash. He then asked those who joined him if anyone needed anything. Several made their selections of shirts, pants and sweaters. When all returned to the smoke shop, other Rastas who were busily at work bantered Rabu for his expensive taste. Nevertheless, a brother felt that it would be a better idea if he, rather than Rabu, wore the suit that very night to an upcoming party. Rabu protested, but finally relented and ceded the use of his suit for the night.

As is common throughout Rastafarian society, women play a minor role in the public life of these Rastas. They are not very visible in the shops and they spend their days at home with the children for the most part. Rabu believes that women can "hold a man back." Although Rabu supports three households, his emotional life seems to be intertwined with the company of male Rastas. Occasionally, Rastas will bring their male children on their jaunts to the shops.

Rashi

Rashi manages an ital food restaurant around the corner from the smoke shop. A backyard route connects his store with the smoke shop, a path that the Rastas use when distributing the herb among their brethren. Rashi entered the United States on a tourist visa but never returned to Jamaica. His restaurant is listed under the ownership of another Rasta. It serves fish, tea, and vegetable patties but no meats or coffee.

Rashi is a masterful storyteller. Inquiries about Rastafarian life are likely to move him to weave narratives about Rastas based on his unique interpretation of the Biblical scriptures. For instance, a favorite tale of his concerns the origin of the peculiar indentation that the red snapper fish allegedly has on its tail. Rashi explains:

"When Christ told his disciples that he would make them fishers of men, he held up a red snapper and from that day on, the red snapper has had the marks of Christ's fingers on its tail. That's why Rastas like red snapper, ital food."

He tells another story explaining the Rasta abstinence from pork.

"Pork is forbidden because Christ cursed the pigs. When he cast out the demons from people, he put them into pigs. Rastas don't want to eat the devil."

Rashi finds that the scriptures prove how timeless Rasta culture is. Despite his Baptist training which taught that the Rastas were evil, Rashi came to Rasta truth because of its "anciency." Thus, he says:

"The Rastas only use ancient things, food, dress, speech and religion. That's why they don't comb their hair. The comb is modern, and not found in the Bible."

Rasta adherence to ital *(natural) food is a distinguishing characteristic of the movement.* (Richard Kenefick)

The ancient origins of the herb also demonstrate Rastas' truth. "Anyone can see how old the weed is. On Solomon's grave grew the weed. When they buried him, it grew all over his grave. You can read that in the Bible. Solomon was wise because he used the weed. It is ancient."

Modernity also undermines the police's claim to authority. "The police? They are moderns. You don't find police in the Bible. Where did they come from? They are always looking for trouble."

Responding to a suggestion that Rasta violence causes the police to harass Rastas, Rashi says: "Rastas do not kill people. Rastas frighten people, yes, but they don't kill people. But the police don't care. They don't want to hear the truth. All flesh and blood are created equal. Equal rights and justice for all."

Rashi limps, a disability he claims came from a bullet wound inflicted by the police in Kingston, Jamaica. The attack occurred at the time of the political campaign in the 1980s when the outlook for Manley, the socialist, seeking reelection, looked dim. Some police officers, evidently in sympathy with the JLP, the opposition party, picked Rashi up at a place called Halfway Tree in Kingston. Since the Rastas had enjoyed some esteem during the Manley regime, this was an opportunity for the frustrated police to vent their emotions on the socialists. They took Rashi downtown, interrogated him, and asked him if he were a Communist or a Cuban spy. While being driven to another precinct, Rashi attempted to escape by dashing from the patrol car while it waited at a traffic light. The police shot him in the leg and shattered his kneecap.

Rashi uses the story about his limp leg as a pedagogical tool to demonstrate how corrupt a people can become through politics. In Jamaica, he says, politics is a way of advancing one's position by courting the favors of the party in power. "If your party is in, rejoice. If it is out, weep!" The political victory of one or the other party, either the JLP or the PNP, brings blessings or afflictions upon people. Rashi is amazed that people don't understand why violence is rampant. Babylon plays its games and the lives of people are at stake.

Baba

Baba is a close friend of Rashi's. He frequently assists Rashi in chores around the restaurant. Baba was born in Jamaica and is not an American citizen. He incorporates the trickster image of Rasta identity very well. He has escaped arrests despite his flagrant violations of the laws against marijuana and various business regulations. Yet, he has persevered in his lifestyle and philosophy. He is a peaceful person in demeanor. Nevertheless, he believes that the injustices in life demand a fierce rhetoric and stance against the establishment. The battle is a chronic one. The following conversation with Baba indicates his commitment to Rasta.

"Why did you become Rasta, Baba?"

"I became a Rasta in Jamaica when I was aware of the differences between the people in the hills and the ghettos downtown. The criminal was the landlord."

"What happened to you in the States since you left Jamaica?"

"I was almost arrested several times for possession of ganja and weapons. I sell ganja for survival."

"Baba, would you waste a cop?"

"I would waste a cop if he does something first."

"You mean if he tries to beat you up?"

"Yes."

"Tell me about another side of Rasta life, the peaceful side."

"The Rastas preserve life, show people how to live, how to eat, how to live peacefully."

"What is the importance of Rasta?"

"The Rastas understand people's needs. Rastas are natural people. The natural people must rule. The natural man is the one who knows what people need."

"So what makes Rasta different from any other religion?"

"Rastas are not talking about heaven but about here. That's what their deal is about."

"But Rastas are involved in criminal activities. How should people accept that?"

"Man has weaknesses. But opportunities come to stop that. A robber may have to do it for survival. But one should start a business after robbery; or even after selling weed, coke, heroin. One has to do it, and then get out of the situation."

"Are not cops guardians of the peace?"

"Cops would just rob Rastas if they could, and for the money."

"So should we legalize ganja?"

"Legalize ganja and you legalize the Rasta wish to turn the place upside down. Legalization of ganja means turning it all upside down."

"Baba, what does it mean to meditate like a Rasta?"

"You meditate with ganja. You think of becoming bigger. That's why ganja cannot be legalized because they want Rastas to think about survival only."

The brief discussion on law and ganja brings the flow of thought to a reflection on Rasta organization, leadership and political involvement.

"Do all Rastas think as you do, Baba?"

"Rastas have many splinter groups. Some Rastas follow Babylonian society. But I am not attracted to them."

"You mentioned that Rastas should form their own communities. But how could they control their behavior?"

"You reason with a man to change. If his behavior is wrong, God is the final judge. The law of the Rastas is the righteous law of the governments, the laws of Moses. But we will need prisons and judges. But Rastas don't have it yet. They are scared. We Rastas are damned with unrighteous rulers as our punishment because we don't get politically involved."

"Yes, but under Manley, many Rastas got involved, and that seemed to be a failure. The Rasta philosophy did not take hold in Jamaican society."

"Manley was bribed. Rastas were bribed by materialism."

"Then what would you do with a leader who is seduced by materialism?"

"I would assassinate any ruler who oppresses people. I would kill him."

"Do you want to be a leader of the community?"

"I need anonymity. I sell. That's why I don't go to the community meetings. Getting arrested is bullshit. That keeps me from my mission.

"Mission?"

"Yes. Reasoning like this with you."

9

Rastas and Symbolic Action

The social interaction of the Rastas with the society around them is best described as a drama. Their presentation of self is dramatic because they enact roles that are thematic variations on their origins in the 1930s. The Rasta conflict with American society, for instance, takes on a dramaturgical perspective as the Rastas relate to the American police through a script that transforms their tensions into rituals. Confrontations between the Rasta and American law enforcement agencies surpass a mere clash between the law and criminals; for the Rasta, these encounters take on redemptive qualities.

Ritual drama is a key to understanding the tensions between the culture of Rastafari and the hegemony of modern, western values. If we look at ritual processes in premodern or nonstate societies, we see that social rituals nourish cultural life because they act as means by which people can scrutinize and satirize their daily experiences. Such ritual dramas transform all the participants. Society returns to a balance, no longer threatened by the possibility of social disruption because of births, marriages, sickness and death (Turner, 1969).

In examining modern society, however, we see that the division of labor has reduced these ritual dramas by channeling them into separate artistic categories such as the theatre, art and poetry. In modern society, redress of grievances or social disturbances can only be handled through these art forms, which are apart from daily life. The use of ritual, or social drama, to mend tears in the cultural

95

fabric would appear anachronistic in a modern, capitalistic society.

The Rastas, however, do enact social drama that ridicules, satirizes and mocks public morality and legal sensibilities masquerading as deep values. In the urban centers of the United States, for example, the Rasta revival of ritual drama is most evident in their conflict with the criminal justice system.

The Police

Since the early 1980s, the police department of one large American city has authorized a specially crafted film to instruct its cadets on the dangers of the Rastafarian movement. For most of the recruits, the film is their only exposure to Rastas before their active duty begins.

The film promotes the premise that many Rastas are guilty of serious crime. Several criminal problems have arisen in this city, and the police intelligence division has traced many of these crimes, which include rape and murder, to what they call the Rastafarian cult. The film links the Rastas' dealing in marijuana with an inherent tendency toward violence which, it claims, is facilitated by their communication networks.

The Rastas' beliefs about the religious use of marijuana are discredited. Police know that Rasta communities grow wealthy on the sale of marijuana. The intelligence division takes this as proof that the Rastas are manipulating religion in order to turn a profit through their illegal activities. Funds and narcotics flow through their distributive networks which the Rastas defend with sophisticated weaponry.

The film's narrator cautions the officers to take special care whenever they confront a Rastafarian. He warns: "Do not become lax in dealing with the Rastafarians. Use all the necessary precautions that one would use when going after a wanted felon. Then you will be relatively safe in dealing with the Rastafarians, and you will not encounter any unnecessary problems. The police officer should not be disarmed by the slight build of the Rastas. Always keep in mind that the Rastas do not respect authority. Remember to look for the hidden 25 caliber [pistol] in his hair."

A detective next interviews a former Rasta. The Rasta offers the following: "A lot of things about Rasta, law enforcement don't know. It's evil, and they should know. The Rastas work in teams. They carry nine millimeters, 45 automatics. By informing on them, I am not betraying them. I am doing what God loves. If the Rastas are confronted by the police, and if it is a position where he can shoot it out, he will do so."

"What can you tell the police?" asks the detective.

"I would say that they be very careful. It's dangerous to turn up on a Rasta, no matter who you are."

The film ends with the warning: "Rastafarians are not to be taken lightly, especially those that appear docile. They will use any means necessary to get away, even shoot you. They have no qualms about firing on an officer. They are good marksmen. Keep in mind that you are dealing with a wanted fugitive. That will guarantee you that you will go home the same way you came to work."

The documentary, then, provides the basis for the intellectual and emotional script that the police officers will use to position themselves in relation to the Rastafarian menace to law and order. The film prods the recruits to increase their fear of Rastas and raise their suspicions about them. Upon viewing it, many officers comment on the resemblance they see between the Rastas and organized crime. They resent the Rasta disrespect for authority and inveigh against their use of marijuana both as sacrament and means of financial aggrandizement. When informed of the contrasting attitude of the Jamaican police, many retorted with charges that the Jamaican police must be corrupt to be so lenient and ambivalent about them.

The script through which the Rastas dramatize their lives is, of course, quite different. The Rastas generate a discourse that legitimizes their experiences within an historical and cultural perspective. This is not simply a response to American law officials nor a denunciation of statutory law as such. Their script flows from what a Rasta lawyer calls "sufferation" and struggle, which, for the Rastas, will continue until the arrival in full of "the natural and righteous law of Jah Rastafari—Selassie I."

In their social drama, the Rastas are rekindling a waning tradition that has ridiculed and satirized legitimate authority. Their behavior shares a likeness with the social drama of the medieval Charivari, "a boisterous mixture of playfulness and cruelty . . . to set things right in a community," the Franciscan movement of the twelfth century, the rowdiness of the religious clowning of the Pueblo Indians, and the Feast of Fools of medieval Europe. The popular press tends to interpret this aspect of Rasta behavior as criminal activity. An English official remarked through the *London Times*: "The Rastas are strong on self-sufficiency. They run their own cooperatives. But until they act responsibly, they won't get credit." Acting responsibly, he added, meant "laying off the ganja." More damaging comments have appeared in American newspapers including the *New York Times*. All linked, without just cause, the culture of Rastafari to organized crime, violence and the drug traffic. What is overlooked in this criticism of the movement is that the Rastas are engaging the antistructural, imaginative and creative behavior that is central to community building.

The culture of Rastafari re-presents to the modern consciousness a social drama that confronts society with the demon, the trickster and the ambiguities in the human personality. The smoke shop in the urban United States, for instance, is one of the stages on which the Rastas play out their social drama. Here their rejection of staid values in anticipation of a new creation, is most threatening. Their smoke shops portend chaos for the neighborhood, troubling West Indian residents with fears that their youth might find their way to Rastafari and embrace the ways of the Rastas.

Urban Rastas

I have already taken note of the dramatic tone of some urban Rastas. Themes are evident: a fearless attitude toward law and authority; gregariousness, a strong conviction of self-worth and a final victory. The Rastas' performance is mimesis, a reliving of an historical memory that recapitulates the passage of the enslaved Africans. As one Rasta poet expressed his sense of identity: "You have got to be the son of an African. You have got to be the son of a slave." They evaluate all contemporary events through the prism of a memory that never forgets the primordial crime, slavery. While their encounters with the law can be traced to the tensions between the Jamaican peasantry and those interested in capitalist development during the 1930s, this secular view of their history does not move the Rastas, who prefer to mythologize their conflicts with the state in ways that satisfy the human need for transcendence. Their interpretation of the scriptures and their confidence in victory provide them the opportunities to redress their history, both as one of suffering and as one moving towards emancipation. Rasta lore reverberates with stories and legends about the Pinnacle, Back-o-Wall, and early founders like Hibbert. These fascinate the Rastas, and eventually Rabu and other contemporary Rastas will enter that lore, even if only on a local scale. The Rasta dialogues, which they call reasoning, celebrate the power of a divinity made flesh in Haile Selassie I and the conquest of life over death, which gives them a view of history from the vantage point of the free and redeemed.

Rasta reasoning sessions create frames of reference that ground the culture of Rastafari, delineating what counts and what does not count. A Rasta cannot take leave of a reasoning session without being transformed into a person ready for a new world. Their reasoning sessions do not fit the bureaucratization, professionalism, urbanization and literacy of contemporary society.

The urban Rastas also enjoy stories about Anancy, African tales that have survived to this day in Jamaica. Anancy's cunning, insight and flexibility assured the god-man-spider of victory over all enemies. After experiencing many trials and tribulations, the Rastas will similarly vanquish their foes.

The major source of conflict between Rastas and society is their dealing in marijuana, although we have seen that they contest the dominance of law and order on other fronts as well. The police film discussed earlier leads to a facile identification of Rastas with the common wheeling and dealing subculture of organized crime. Is this true? Can "brute nature," the pursuit of pleasure as a means of escaping bureaucratized society, be applied to the Rasta? In fact, one would be hard pressed to discover brute nature compelling Rastas' activities. Their behavior departs significantly from the motivational basis of the ordinary wheeler and dealer, for hedonism does not appear to be at the core of their lifestyle. Sheer materialism, greed and the love of pleasure have been observed among organized criminals, but this has not been as readily observed among Rastas. Indeed quite the opposite is true of the Rastas, as Ras and the others reveal to the observer. Their perspective on history, their memory of the past and expectations for the future, put them beyond the subjectivity of an individualized brute nature seeking gratification and pleasure.

What is the text the Rastas employ? Their rhetoric, their exclusion of women from the male groupings, and even their enjoyment of Bruce Lee movies on a Saturday afternoon around the television set, are parts of their texts. Their text begins in the smoke shops and in their reasoning about themselves. Their indifference toward the police, anticipation of their raids, and, of course, their stints in jail become the stages for the enactment of that text in a dramatized way.

The Rastas represent disorder, but they are not nihilists. As modern tricksters, they too have an ethical message. They criticize nearly everything the bourgeois world holds sacred: its God, social classes, scientization of drugs and justifications for poverty. Their constant clash with the law and public opinion is legendary. Here the Rastas are the social dramatists who challenge the legal, medical and social systems that the bourgeois world has created in the courts, in the neighborhoods and in capitalist and socialist business adventures. The texture of Rasta lives sets them apart from the dominant society as well as from the pleasure-seeking subculture of the drug trade. The wheelers and dealers of the organized drug trade arrange their lives around a strategy of rational calculation whose purpose is to avoid detection and arrest. If they are arrested, they attribute such misfortune to their own negligence and failure to observe routine precautions. Too much talk, too much drink, a too carefree attitude towards the business of the drug trade, that is what they believe eventually causes their entrapment by the law. If they should escape arrest, they believe it is because of the ineptitude and stupidity of the police. The Rastas, on the other hand, frame their conflict with the law in a history of redemption.

Rasta Dramatic Ritual and the Law

Rabu and the other Rastas have devised scenarios which meet the oppression of the law in a way which distinguishes them from the ordinary pleasure-seeking criminal. They fashion bits and pieces from their symbolic world into the creation of a street theatre that mediates the tensions between themselves and the police. Fueling their drama is not rational calculation to beat the system but the hastening toward an apocalyptic future and freedom. The police, on their part, view their role in this simply as the guardians of law and order.

The Rastas are quite familiar with the script the police follow. Their interaction with the law has been orchestrated ever since their feisty origins in the 1930s. Whatever conflicts the Rasta experience in American neighborhoods are only a recapitulation of the strife between Babylon and those who have a covenant with Jah Rastafari. More so than the police, the Rastas see that all people must play a role that flows from the social niche that they occupy. One is the way of Babylon, and the other is an embrace of Jah Rastafari in one's flesh. The "shitism" of Babylon brings them strife, but this interaction with Babylon is also the opportunity to sharpen their wits and cunning for the final victory.

The occasions when the police raid the Rasta smoke shops are moments of ritual confrontation between opposing forces. Axes chop up the shops. Tables are overturned. Sewing machines are toppled. Dry goods are ripped from the shelves and unrolled carelessly. Cassettes, films and radios are all confiscated as evidence. Finally, the cache of marijuana is uncovered. The deed is done. Yet, the Rastas remain sullen and quiet during the onslaught. They feign ignorance and put up no defense. "You have the right to remain silent. . . ."

Later the Rastas will say that "thus it has been, and thus it will always be, until Jah's people conquer." The raids are the inevitable consequence of their sojourn in Babylon. Inevitably they shrug off the raids, no matter how damaging they may have been to their personal property. "That's the cops' job. They must raid us, but we will win in the end." The Rastas will even anticipate the raids on their smoke shops. Thus, some think it is a good idea to always be prepared for the stint with a good meal because Rasta food is not served in jail.

The police marvel at the naivete of the Rastas' enterprises. They are easy targets and launch their businesses as if they were invulnerable to law enforcement. The Rastas, however, do not perceive themselves as hapless victims of evil.

The Rastas' script is meant to deceive. The police raid the Rastas' smoke shops but then occurs the dramatic unfolding of a truth that the Rastas believe is known only by themselves. In America the Rastas are jailed, their smoke shops raided, and their locks shaved by authorities. Yet, the brethren endure, as they always have. Ashi and the other Rastas interpret their comings and goings as if they were entrances and exits onto a stage that is revealing a significant truth. Whatever happens has been written into the dialogue long before the present time. The Rastas are indifferent to their confrontations with the law, for this is a way of confirming their identity. Just as Moses led Pharaoh's troops to destruction in the sea when they pursued the Chosen People, so will it be for all of Babylon's forces.

The police told me that their raids on the smoke shops deter and discourage the Rastas. This is what the Rastas wish the police to believe. They purposely provide a space in which the police officer can exercise authority and feel in control of the situation. The raids do pressure the Rastas into tightening controls over the sale of ganja so that everything looks respectable. These controls may take the form of excluding children from any business transactions as well as seeing to it that buyers are dispersed from the store fronts. The Rastas know that too much trade will only taunt the police and any unseemly spectacle in front of the stores will offend the neighbors. True to their Jamaican experiences, the Rastas want to appear as respecters of the law.

We would miss another point of the drama, however, if we forget that the Rastas create their dramatic selves for the sake of the audience in the larger community around them. These selves are based on the role of the self-sufficient but persecuted Rasta. The

Rastas wish to present themselves as paradigms for new lifestyles. Law officials may raid their shops and keep them under surveillance. Yet, they are also a people who work, care for their children, and look out for one another's welfare with as much vigilance as any other group in the community. Their shops are even places of conviviality for neighborhood males. Their lifestyle is not that of the self-seeking and hedonistic underground drug culture depicted by the police.

Dramatic Resolution

The dramatic conflict between the Rastas and the police indicates turmoil between the two which has been translated into a police training film about the menace of Rastafari. The abstract has become the particular. What mediates between the police, the Rastas and the law to create conflict of dramatic proportions is a script that both have created. The script for the police is the subjectivity with which the officers confront the objective fact of the Rastas' illegal behavior. An officer may justify his or her behavior on the premise that they "play the game" with the Rastas in order to apprehend the strong men behind the scene. But actually, in the dramatic conflict between the police and the Rastas there is a social exchange that perpetuates itself. This conflict as a social exchange has advantages for both police and the Rastas, as we have seen.

However, in the mid-1980s the conflict came to an unanticipated resolution. What caused the cessation of dramatic conflict, at least for a time, was the suppression of local knowledge that the police were employing to monitor the situation. In its stead was introduced the expertise of outside narcotic agents, who pressured the local precincts to be more effective in undermining the drug trade. More pressure was used against the Rastas—more arrests, more fines, more raids, and more destruction of property. Under orders from the higher echelons of authority who were outside the neighborhood, police officers were compelled to strike at Rastas' shops more devastatingly than before. These constraints made the maintenance of the shops impossible for the Rastas. One sensed that the local police were not really in charge of the situation, since outside authorities were "calling the shots." During this time, the Rastas took steps to demonstrate that their shops were engaging in legitimate business, such as the selling of reggae records, leather goods, and so on. One shop even went so far as to post a handwritten sign on the front door reading "No herb sold here." Nevertheless, it was obvious that the brethren were still enjoying the "smoke" amongst themselves.

When the pressures from above relented and the narcotic agents turned their attention to the cocaine and heroin traffic, the Rastas reopened their smoke shops. Then the police returned to acting on their local knowledge, and the script was played out once again. This time around, however, the Rastas were more cautious in their dealings, and their crises with the law took place without serious overt confrontations. The police complain that they know what is going on in those stores but will wait another day to raid them. We should not take this to mean that the Rastas are having it their own way. They are not. They are raided. Shops are closed and some Rastas are hauled off to jail. Nevertheless, their presence in the neighborhood persists and there is a mutual social recognition between themselves and the local police.

The opening and closing of the Rasta businesses creates an "irreparable schism" between themselves and the police that continues to have meaning in their symbolic life. Haile Selassie, Babylon, and the Rastas' "new Zions" are themes which consistently emerge as they interpret their experience with the law. Their social deportment has a dramaturgical perspective because of this special interpretation, which carries the weight of redemptive action. The Rastas believe that they will ultimately prevail in the United States just as they believe they will prevail on the beach in southern Jamaica and in their commune at Bull Bay. This confidence in their redemption will continue until such time as the state bureaucracy, frustrated by the slowness of its resolution of the Rasta "problem," takes swifter and harsher actions against them.

Viewing the conflict between Rastas and the American police as a dramatic confrontation allows us to glean insights into the differences and similarities between Jamaican law enforcement and its counterpart in the United States. The pluralism of Jamaican society allows a multiplicity of religious, political and philosophical viewpoints and interpretations of events. This pluralism permits a mutual acceptance of the schisms and social dramas played out between the Rastas and other social groups. However, at the national level in our modern industrialized society, with its respect for learning, literacy and individualism, a more rational, "impartial" approach is taken to settle differences.

In the United States, at the national level of law enforcement, the same law is applied to everyone, and the guardians of our criminal justice system refuse to distinguish between Rastas selling marijuana and other "garden variety" dealers in the drug. On the other hand, where there is no national intervention, the "Rasta problem" may be handled by local police acting on local knowledge and "playing the game" with the Rasta. Where police use their local knowledge to address the Rastas, there is mutual acceptance of the long, drawn out, irrevocable conflict, each side with its own "script," which may be truly called social drama.

American society in general attempts either to rationalize or discredit the Rastas on psychological or economic grounds. Either the Rastas are viewed as adolescent personalities who will shed their beliefs as they become mature adults adjusted to society, or they are viewed as the deprived poor demanding their share of the wealth. This American perspective contrasts with the Jamaican one, where ritualized drama is the norm for dealing with the endless conflict between the Rastas and the legal apparatus. In Jamaica, for example, where the Rastas dispute the claims of bureaucracies such as the Urban Development Corporation to their squatters' land, the Rastas do not challenge the state through the courts. They know that at this time, popular Jamaican sentiment is on their side. For the moment the Rasta are content that Jamaican society utilizes local knowledge about them which distinguishes their lifestyle from that of other Jamaicans, and accords it a certain legitimacy. In other words, unlike the United States, where the courts and legal action are considered the most desirable way to deal with the Rastas, in Jamaica, social drama still prevails.

10

Repatriation

In the mid-sixties, under the auspices of the Jamaican government, a group of Rastafari visited several African states in order to find a suitable place for the brethren to repatriate. On their itinerary was Ethiopia, the precapitalist and feudalistic kingdom of Emperor Haile Selassie I. Impressed by their mission, Haile Selassie granted them land in Shashemene, a crossroads town in the southern Shoa Province. By the end of the sixties some of the Rastafari migrated from Jamaica and settled on that fertile Ethiopian land, where they now cultivate the grains for which the region is known, and engage in animal husbandry.

Shashemene is an agricultural town with about 13,000 inhabitants that lies 250 kilometers south of Addis Ababa. It was a garrison town built by the imperialistic Amharic dynasty at the end of the nineteenth century in order to subdue the tribal peoples. The Amharic are the dominant ethnic group in the area. The other traditional ethnic groups are the Oromo, Gurage and Welayita who live in the rural areas outside of town but visit and trade at the daily market in Shashemene. Shashemene is 90 percent Christian and 10 percent Muslim.

The economic base for the town is in transport, trade and farming. The peasants cultivate maize, beans, potatoes, wheat, barley and t'ef, a local grain used in the traditional Ethiopian bread called injera. From the bus terminal in town one can travel to all the major cities in southern Ethiopia. Much informal economic activity, not controlled by the state, takes place in the daily market.

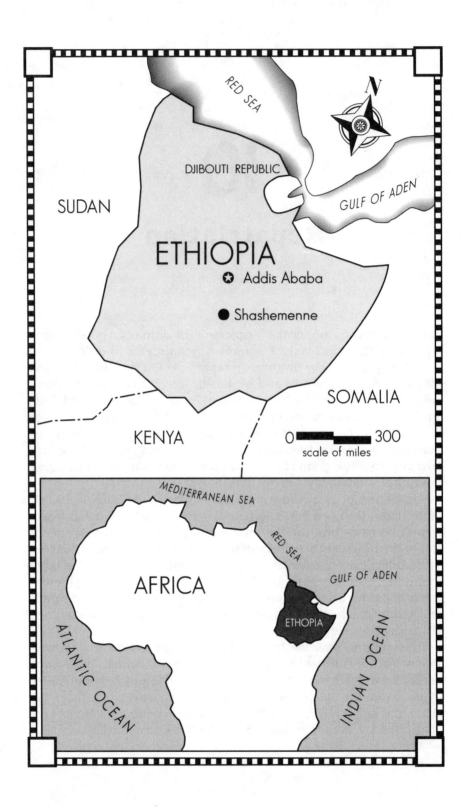

Ethiopian markets are economic and social centers. (United Nations)

Shashemene is a truck stop where drivers pause overnight on their long haul to Addis loaded with coffee and other food products from the South. The town bristles with life. Bars line the main street; dilapidated hotels buzz with weary travellers, and sexual liaisons are easy to find. It is a place, too, where men ordinarily associate with men and women with women in prescribed forms of etiquette and respect. The division between the sexes is so strict that mingling between them can only mean sexual intent in the eyes of the beholders. A foreigner to the town, where the rate of venereal disease, which carries no stigma, is almost 90 percent, would have no difficulty enjoying the favors of its women. Prostitution is a lucrative profession whose profits can lead to a woman's ownership of a bar, an opportunity much more advantageous than marriage.

In the center of town is the daily market where agricultural and other products can be purchased in bulk. Butter, a favorite skin softener and hair conditioner, spices and textiles from the South are plentiful. Here too, one can easily purchase *chat*, a plant stimulant whose leafiness gives it a resemblance to the vegetable arugula. The stimulant is a favorite among the Muslims who prohibit alcoholic drink. The Christians prefer the Ethiopian beer and consider chat to induce madness in its users. Some Christian friends showed me pictures of Muslims who had supposedly gone mad under the influence of the plant. The marketplace is also the working ground for thieves. I was warned to avoid confrontations with anyone there because this might be a set-up for a group of thieves to steal from me. Indeed, I was jostled in the marketplace, but my guides deftly steered me away from such encounters.

Most interesting about the Ethiopian culture in recent times are the changes that were introduced by the Marxist revolution of 1974. The Marxist regime that emerged under Haile Mariam Mengistu transformed Ethiopia from a feudalistic state into a socialist one. After the deposition of Haile Selassie and his royal retinue, the aristocracy was stripped of power and privilege, and lands were placed under the management of the peasants. Peasants' associations, rather than individual ownership, prevailed. The peasants were required to sell their surplus to the Agricultural Marketing Corporation at a fixed low price. Under Mengistu the peasants' debts were cancelled and they were freed of the requirement to pay rent to a landlord. Then they were better able to feed themselves although they never became prosperous.

In an effort to rationalize the economy and move the peasantry away from a subsistence economy, the socialist state required the peasants to devote certain hours of their labor time to the state farms. The state rewarded the peasants for their efforts, not with money but with symbolic praises for their labor in the form of medals or certificates of citation. Productive peasants were extolled for their contribution to the success of the revolution. Peasants were required to join neighborhood associations or *Kebeles* where they gather together periodically for instructions on the Marxist theories of progress, justice and prosperity. The officials conducted these meetings during the times of religious observance on Sundays in an attempt to wean the peasants from their dependency on religious values. The Ethiopian peasant often views misfortunes such as drought to be a visitation from God and the state sees this sentiment as injurious to development. Moreover, not only was religion seen to interfere with the secular goals of the Marxist government, but tribal interests and traditional ways of justice were perceived in this negative way as well.

When I was conducting my fieldwork in Shashemene in 1986, the drought that had brought suffering to the area a year before was only a memory. The rains had returned and food relief from the United States and other nations was available throughout the area.

The socialist Ethiopian state gathered peasants like this man together in neighborhood associations and rewarded productivity. (United Nations)

The missionaries had acted as efficient distributors of the relief supplies for the town. The southern provinces had benefited far more from famine relief than their rebellious neighbors to the north in Eritrea. However, the steady stream of food relief presented a problem for the authorities because its abundance prompted many of the peasants to work less in the fields.

Antonio: A Repatriated Rasta

My first encounter with the Rastafari brethren occurred in the daily market of Shashemene. My casual conversation with a Rasta named Antonio led to an invitation to visit their compound about three miles from the open market. I noticed how hurriedly the brethren conducted their business in the market. They did not display the ceremonious behavior that was common among the tribal peoples who traded there.

North of the center of town the Rastafari community dots the main road leading from Shashemene to Addis. Here are the Twelve Tribes of Israel, branches of which exist also in New York City and Jamaica. They build their houses with the traditional materials—mud, straw, clay and a loose concrete mixture. The walls of their houses are very porous which, they say, allows them to breathe. These materials will last forever. However, they will not build above the second floor because they know that this would be entering God's realm and defying him. The scriptures prove this with the narrative about the tower of Babel.

Antonio emphasized the importance of the Twelve Tribes, for this is the only formalized expression of Rastafari. In a somewhat sectarian manner, he asked rhetorically how one could claim to be Rastafari without an affiliation with the Twelve Tribes.

Antonio is a repatriated African who heaps praise on his new found freedom in Shashemene. He felt compelled to flee the Babylonian system of Jamaica by the demands of his own salvation. Any compromise with the system would have been deadly. Repatriation to Africa was then a redemptive act. Here land was plentiful and a man did not have to rely on the system of wage labor for food, shelter and clothing. Indeed, the informal economic system to which the Shashemene brethren subscribed not only avoided surveillance by the state but also cultivated a sense of freedom.

In his commune, Antonio boasts of no class division. The most competent men lead the work projects: electricians, plumbers and master builders. They are completely self-sufficient.

When I inquired about theological matters in Rastafari, such as what I perceived to be its lack of dogma and authority, Antonio chastised me with his eschatology. "This is no longer a time for discussion on this or that perspective on the Rastafari. Time is short. By the year 2000 all things will be destroyed in the West. The talks on nuclear disarmament are useless. Satan sits at the conference table. Only repatriation makes sense."

"How does one disengage from the system?" I wondered aloud.

This question had puzzled me during my sojourn among the brethren in Brooklyn and Jamaica, and it returned here. Antonio explained that independence meant a separation from any system that is beyond the control of the brethren. Autonomy and self-sufficiency are the means for disengaging from a diabolical system of economic and political control. In stating this, Antonio reminded me very much of one Rasta, Prince, in Brooklyn, who held to the same principle.

The days passed and I met three brethren whom I had not encountered on any previous visit to the compound. Nevertheless, they were quite informed about my visit to Shashemene and seemed perturbed that I was residing at the local Catholic mission. I was soon to learn the reason why.

These brethren were dogmatic about the divinity of His Majesty Haile Selassie I, although they felt it was dangerous to believe such things in the present state of affairs. For them, the end was coming and no one had time to debate issues. The Pope was Satan. The divinity of His Majesty was all pervasive. Where did I stand in all of this?

Since I had not converted to their way of life, their suspicions of me grew by the minute. They insisted that I remain with them in Shashemene, abandon the Catholic priesthood and become a member of the Twelve Tribes, all of this to prove my friendship with Rastafari! Again and again they pummelled me with accusations that my interest in Rastafari was only academic until I became a member of the commune.

They scoffed at my suggestion that I could be a friend of the brethren. Pointing out the freedom that I felt in my heart did not appease them. They rejected my overtures to make them into an object of investigation. Instead they turned the vision of objectivity on me, and I became the object of scrutiny. What did they understand that had escaped me?

Later, after much reflection, I realized that my commitment to the priesthood was a highly rational and intellectual one. It was indeed involved with an abstraction rather than a concrete commitment toward the building of community. I was an intellectual whose theology was more a matter of academic pursuit than one of liberation. The brethren rightly sensed that this was the manner in which I was grasping Rastafari. If I made the brethren into an object of intellectual scrutiny, it was because this is how I had learned to legitimize my own religious conviction.

An Amharic Woman

Soon I inquired from the missionaries about an Amharic woman who was formerly a wife of a Rastafari brother at Shashemene. The Catholic missionaries arranged our meeting which took place about 30 miles north of Shashemene where she resided at a mission station. She had lived with her husband for four years and then broke the marriage. Exasperated after he locked her and her daughter in a back room, she fled the commune.

This woman found the Rastafari way of life too oppressive for her Ethiopian sensibilities. The Rastas' poor treatment of women and the incongruity of their lifestyle with the Ethiopian rhythms of life caused her to reject them. Infractions of the rules imposed by the male-dominated commune often resulted in beatings and injuries to the women. She showed me the scars she bore from such a beating when she was punished for lingering too long in the daily market. Her husband had carefully timed her trips to the market and lateness aroused suspicions of infidelity.

She smiled when she related how the men spent long hours reading the scriptures, smoking ganja and praising Haile Selassie. They listened to the BBC to interpret world events with their own cosmic significance. At night they saw visions in their dreams of things that would come to pass. When I mentioned that many Muslim men in Shashemene use the drug "quat" (chat), she responded that this was for pleasure. The Rastafari used ganja for more serious purposes than mere pleasure, for it was like the consecrated bread in the Holy Liturgy. She continued. "The Jamaicans (as the people of Shashemene call them) smoke ganja constantly. They prefer to use this over any other medical cure. Yet they are very strong and clean with great concern about personal hygiene. They eat no meat and do not eat Ethiopian foods. No coffee or tea; only fish tea. They will not allow their Ethiopian wives to follow any Ethiopian customs in their kitchens."

She explained how the Rastafari are Jamaicans. They are not Ethiopians whose gentility and manners are matters of ritualized etiquette. Indeed, I recalled that within the marketplace, the brethren never displayed the demeanor and ritual greetings that mark the daily deportment of an Amharic male. To the Amharic, they appeared gruff, short-tempered and poorly tuned to the pace of the Amharic peasant.

The economic base of the Rastafari commune is very informal. Jamaicans from home support them and they are often aided by the Jamaican consulate in Addis. They certainly do not work for wages but tend to keep to themselves. This woman claimed that newcomers to the commune are soon disillusioned. After staying there and contributing their money to the brethren, they lose heart and leave. The newcomers, she claimed, are exploited and overworked through a process which the brethren call education. If they remain, it is because the brethren put fear in their hearts that the Twelve Tribes in Jamaica will shoot them should they leave. To return to Babylon is forbidden and sacrilegious.

An important source of money raising is letter writing. The leaders of the commune send letters to Jamaicans, she said, telling them of the beauties in the community. In response, Jamaicans become interested in their cause and send them money. This behavior reminded me of the poor in Jamaica who would befriend someone from the States and later on send the person "begging letters."

This Amharic woman had no regrets about leaving the commune. Yet the brethren were always trying to persuade her to return. She feared retaliation. She concealed our conversation from her daughter because she did not want her to carry tales back to her father in Shashemene. Her father taught the girl things about the Rastafari way of life like painting Rastafari inspired pictures. He himself enjoyed painting the likeness of Haile Selassie for hours on end. His wife found this a silly practice and another reason for leaving.

Her experience with the Rastafari was truly an unhappy one. She did not understand their hatred for the Babylonian oppressor. It was so intense, she said, that they reproduced photos from magazines that depict the slave trade. These they spread among the community as proof of the whites' oppression of the Africans. Yet, their dislike for the white race was a curious position in Shashemene. In general the relationship between the Ethiopians and the white Italian missionaries was a beneficent one. Further, the Italian invasion of the 1930s did not result in the enslavement of the people and today Italy and Ethiopia enjoy cordial relations. Hence, the justified rhetoric of the western black in the diaspora does not correlate with the lived experience of Ethiopians.

A young Amharic male, companion to this former wife of the Rastafari brother, mentioned to me that he thought the Jamaicans were very nervous. He saw no reason for me to be interested in them. "When they become angry, they are quick to grab a knife and start a fight with the one who is bothering them." He believed that the Jamaicans didn't even like each other. "Everyone in Shashemene knows," he said, "that they live on donations from abroad and sell the clothes they receive as charitable donations in the open market." Their culinary habits were strange to him as well. After collecting bones from slaughterhouses, they made soup from them. To the Amharic people they appeared to be using the bones for evil rituals.

When my several months' sojourn among the Rastafari in Shashemene ended, I concluded that the Rastafari were alone in this ancient land. Their symbolic world which spoke of African roots, blackness and rejection of the white Jesus and racism appeared muted in this Christian and Muslim community of Shashemene. The contributions that they have made in western society through their beliefs, art and music were overshadowed by the venerable cultures of the people around them.

After his visit to Shashemene, one insightful visitor wrote of the Shashemene commune as a rebellion against being outsiders, a way of life maintained by people trying to get inside—not inside the Ethiopian culture but inside themselves. This is very suggestive, for I believe that the Rastafari are indeed outsiders to the Ethiopian style of life. They resist the traditions around them by creating their own enclave in a peasant community. In a real sense they rebel against being non-Ethiopian by creating an African identity that emerges from inside themselves.

In the Marxist state the Rastafari remained indifferent to the aspirations of the proletarian revolution. The distinctive feature of the Rastafari lay elsewhere than in the workers' liberation movement. It rested in their possibility for universalizing the issue of freedom beyond the particularistic interests of industrial workers or wage earners. In other words, the demands of the Rastafari in Shashemene are not oriented toward any instrumental objective such as the seizure of political power. Instead they want a field of autonomy and independence.

I returned from Shashemene to Addis during a heavy downpour. It was the rainy season. The lightning flashed horizontally across the night sky. For one last time I turned to see the commune illumined by that fierce lightning and awash in the flooding rains. My thoughts were sullen. Here were the remnants of the Garveyites, the Pan-Africanists, and those oppressed by the racist system of the West. Had history soiled their vision with its economic and political contradictions? Once friends of the Emperor, the revolution caused the Rastafari to lose the privileges they enjoyed, as if they had been aristocrats. They enjoyed no unique position as newcomers, for newcomers were not unusual in this area. This place had been visited by migrants under the banner of the Ethiopian World Federation as early as the 1930s. The Twelve Tribes were only the latest arrivals, and originally, in the late 1960s, they had been a much larger group than the present inhabitants. These brethren were keeping a part of western history in memory that many bourgeois Jamaicans would rather forget. They struggle more, here in Shashemene, than perhaps they would in a western urban environment. But they are sincere in their stance, indomitable and undaunted. They have no middle-class defenses here, no reliance on the state, welfare or equal opportunity employers. Babylon seemed very far away. Yet I chose to return.

11

Legal Tensions

Accounting for the variety of factions in the Rastafarian movement at this time can be overwhelming, and there are those who bemoan the changes the Rastafarian identity has undergone since the 1930s and 1940s. Some aspects of Rasta's manifold diversity involve ethnic enclaves while others point to a niche amidst the bourgeois codes of modern society. Seeking to identify the true Rasta among the many heretics may be a romantic and even fruitless quest.

Rastas as an Ethnic Group

Ethnicity is a cognitive category based on the presumed biological, social and cultural origins of a particular human group. In considering ethnicity it is important to remember that the identity system of the ethnic actors themselves is highly significant. Ethnic groups tend to exempt the competitive marketplace from impacting on their economic and noneconomic decisions. Then language, food, music, religious beliefs and myths will provide emotional ties to economic interests.

The Rastas who avoid wage labor and depend on communal ties for the production and distribution of wealth are creating ethnic bondings. Examples of these groups in Jamaican society are the commune at Bull Bay, the fishing community on the beach near Kingston, and even the independently reclusive Nigel. They resist the hegemony of the working class and market by standing outside

115

of the pool of employed or unemployed labor. The impersonal and competitive networks of class identity are objects of scorn in their reasoning sessions, for they rely on their Rastafarian beliefs to support the material basis of their lives. Selassie I, repatriation, and black self-worth are some symbols that buttress their material world. Similarly, they do not acknowledge the world of rational calculation in pursuit of profit. For all intents and purposes, the commune at Bull Bay and the fishing village recast a direction toward ethnicity, as witnessed earlier in the 1940s by the commune at Pinnacle. However, the waning of a communal identity and the entrance into the marketplace by other Rastas in middle-class Jamaica and the United States raise some questions.

The argument has been advanced that the strengthening of social class in advanced capitalistic societies reduces the significance of ethnicity in the public sphere. The production and distribution of goods and services no longer depend on the affective ties of ethnic identity. Strategies of productivity and profit occur on a national scale rather than on the local, particularistic scale of the ethnic group. Rational choices are made to undergird the economic system that leave little chance for ethnicity, race, or privilege to propel the economy. Herein rests the free market of capitalism that unhitches the worker from communal ties and obligations and subjects the worker to the domination of the capitalist. The implications of this change may be summarized as follows:

> The central problems of our society have to do, not with ethnic grouping, but with economic policy, social rule, class relations. Towards problems of this kind and magnitude, what answers can ethnicity offer? Very weak ones, I fear. (Steinberg 1981)

The decline of ethnicity and cultural pluralism as well, in advanced capitalist societies coincides with the rise of a sense of national destiny and one people. As the necessity for economic progress captures the public imagination, the material basis in people's lives rather than the ethnic one takes precedence. In the place of family, ethnicity and cultural group, a new understanding of the self comes forth in the form of a national and patriotic identity. The ethnic group no longer provides the context for work and economic advantage. Contracts, wages and labor unions begin to dominate life and the pursuit of goods and services. Any attempt to replace these structures with the ways of ethnic groups and subcultures appears backward, indolent and anarchistic. Furthermore, those who have enjoyed the benefit of capitalist development argue that self-identification on the basis of ethnicity tends to undermine the humanist values of universalism, equality and freedom. These values produce a legal edifice which protects the public realm, and its discourse promotes universal and equal justice before the law. In an advanced capitalist society, then, the function of law is to provide checks on the meaning of justice that ethnicity has developed.

In advanced capitalist societies, some Rastas confront the law not only because they violate the Dangerous Drugs Act but also because they accumulate wealth through methods that by-pass the market. This confrontation is inevitable according to some observers of jurisprudence in the capitalist societies of the West. For these, the system of criminal law is intricately related to economic efficiency and market conditions. Thus:

> The substantive doctrines of the criminal law . . . can be given an economic meaning and can indeed be shown to promote efficiency. . . . The major function of criminal law in a capitalistic society is to prevent people from bypassing . . . the market. . . . Market bypassing in such situations is inefficient. (Posner 1985)

The ethnic identity of Rastas is seriously undermined in such a context, and the pressures to conform are strong. However, it has been argued that ethnicity has a strong function to play in societies where social class formations are underdeveloped. This insight has direct application to the position of the Rastafarian subculture in Jamaican society.

The rational pursuit of economic gain and the hegemony of a working-class culture turned to the directives of the market have not quite penetrated every aspect of life in Jamaica. Although the powerful elite propagate ideologies among the lower classes which legitimize the elite's position in society, other values contradict that ideology. That is, the rationalism of a market economy finds its opposition in values that are rooted in ethnic and cultural identities and hierarchies. Accordingly, Jamaicans may differentiate their status through the amount of privacy they enjoy, whether they live on quiet streets or noisy lanes, whether they enjoy mental and manual labor, and the level of religious restraint or religious ecstasy they allow. These are values that dominate many areas of distribution in Jamaican economic life other than those, such as the dollar value of possessions, that are associated with market exchange.

Where this is so, where ethnic values exist, there is no need for the systematic development of criminal law described above, at least with regard to the efficiency demonstrated in advanced capitalist settings. But uncertainty abounds in Jamaican society about how one is to acquire wealth. On the one hand, there are the folk with their imagination, intuition and ethnic demands for reciprocity, while, on the other, there are the strategies of unionization and collective bargaining, in short, the ways of the market. Interestingly, Jamaica has not developed a mythology around its rich and famous to the extent that the United States has idolized the personalities of the Rockefellers, the Morgans and the Vanderbilts. These personages may symbolize capitalist ingenuity, but one is hard pressed to find similarities in Jamaican folklore where resistance to the psychological residue of slavery and colonialism are celebrated in the same way. Jamaicans do not respond to capitalist categories and the free market with as much alacrity as do Americans. In Jamaica, political maneuvering through patronage, for example, is sufficient to justify the acquisition of wealth, irrational and corrupt as this may be in the judgment of the citizenry in advanced capitalist societies.

In this context, Rastas have legitimacy, and their ethnicity is but their way of gaining wealth among a population with similar tactics. This is so because Jamaicans do not perceive stratifications and identity along class lines but along social and cultural ones as well. Here racial and ethnic factors play prominent roles in social change, along with trade unions, strikes and other, directly economic measures, though a persuasive symbolic apparatus to support capitalist interests is missing. Indeed, in the mid-1980s the government implored the people to avoid holding public protests because that behavior was interfering with the tourist trade, the primary industry of Jamaica. The readiness of some Jamaicans to undermine their own market economy is difficult to understand for those in capitalist societies, who defend their rights through unions, legal challenges in court, and other strategies that enhance rather than deter the growth of the market.

Some Rastas may seek to acquire wealth through their communal identity and inherent rights as descendants of slaves and the oppressed of a greedy Babylon, truths resounding throughout non-Rasta Jamaican folklore as well. Behavior such as trading in marijuana thus becomes valuable to the Rastas because they justify the use and selling of the herb as members of a cultural group. They do not act as members of a social class for whom anything that earns a profit is reasonable. The latter value is the provenance of organized crime, and the former that of ethnicity.

All of this points to the cultural mediation through which many Jamaicans and Americans perceive the Rastas. An advanced capitalist society such as the United States evaluates the Rastas against a legal system that protects the strategies for market gains.

This premise means that, when the Rastas take on respectable behavior such as wage labor, unionization and capital investment, they will gain acceptance and prestige. The more they deviate from this cultural pattern, the less likely is their chance for accommodation in American society. As we have seen earlier, law enforcement agents in America are prone to stigmatize the Rastas as potential criminals. This tendency reflects the capitalist ethos which perceives people's status in terms of economic categories and enshrines those categories in its criminal justice system. In contrast with Jamaican society, Rastas in the United States are readily classified as deviants and threats to the civil order. In short, Americans find the manner in which the Rastas redress their grievances against a hierarchical and stratified society to be repugnant to their sense of how such issues should be settled.

Rastas and Law

Ras, whom we met earlier, mocks the authority of the law because he views it as set on destroying and confiscating the merchandise "of the Rastafari family and their place of business because they seek no friendship with black people at all." Rabu also complains about the authority of the law because it gives the police the power to seize not only their marijuana but also to snatch other property like cameras, televisions, and dry goods. These Rastas chafe against statutory law and find in it an oppressive burden. Two questions arise: How then can Rastas trust the law?, and Why can't these Rastas participate in the legal rationality of an advanced capitalist system?

The immediate response is that these Rastas use a linguistic and symbolic world to wean themselves away from dependence on a belief in social mobility and the rights adhering to private ownership. In other words, although one may argue that the Rastas ultimately must rely on the labor market, their location in it is peculiar. This fact has intellectual, emotive and social consequences. Where a group such as the Rasta have located themselves in different labor market conditions, there develops a different scheme of coding and decoding human activity as well as qualitatively distinct thought processes and communicative skills. Thus, while workers in the primary market, that is, the bureaucracies of the state and industry, develop symbols that are congruent with legal rationality and the purposeful action it commends, others, and these include some Rastas, develop different systems of relevancies and shared meanings. Consequently, the

Two influential Rastas in the Rasta nation declared in the U.S. Virgin Islands. (UPI/Bettman)

legal system judges the stories that Rastas offer to justify their behavior as incredible, an assumption expediting their guilt. Haile Selassie, the conquering lion of the tribes of Judah, repatriation, the healing properties of ganja and the justice inherent in reciprocity may be local relevancies, but in the eyes of formal law, they do not justify illegal activities. The Rastas' dealing with marijuana, their disrespect of police and their underground economy, leave them with no defense. Indeed, formal legal rationality must thwart any tendency in the system to particularize justice in that fashion.

In the United States, for example, Rule 610 of the Federal Rules of Evidence curtails the influence of the subject's culture in determining the gravity of an offense. The rule forbids religious beliefs from being introduced as evidence into a case so that the witness's credibility is enhanced or impaired. Thus, in a 1977 case on the Virgin Islands, Rule 610 was invoked against a move to introduce the beliefs of a Rasta as evidence because this would have prejudiced the proceedings in favor of the defendant. Similarly, a

New York lawyer could not introduce evidence suggesting that adherence to the tenets of Rastafarian culture might diminish the seriousness of an offense committed by a Rasta. Here formal legal rationality creates the legal facts that are beyond the authority of the local group to decide. Instead, the principles that govern the situation in deciding the facts are autonomous, general and universal. This legal attitude de-situates the concrete conditions surrounding behavior and subsumes them under the meanings that legal rationality creates. The interpretations that responsible agents attach to their behavior are then not important in the context of a violated law.

The implications of the discussion thus far bear on the question of the possible accommodation for the Rastas in advanced capitalist societies such as the United States. Anthropologist Clifford Geertz once observed that the current manipulation of the legal process has hindered any kind of legal pluralism in the United States. As he wrote: "the how-to bias of practiced law, how to keep out of courts, if you can, or how to prevail there if you cannot, has kept legal pluralism at bay (Geertz 1983). In light of the "mask of confrontation" that some Rastas may wear, can the United States allow legal pluralism of such a proportion that the group's ethical, emotional, political and practical considerations are paramount? The concept of legal pluralism implies the mutual justification of both the symbolic and material structures of differing cultural groups without thereby endangering the rights of any group to the resources of society. Although we may think that the legal accommodation which has been made for the members of the Native American Church, who use peyote, provides a precedent for this type of legal pluralism, closer examination reveals something else.

The Native American Church in the American southwest received a dispensation from the Dangerous Drugs law. Through this grant its members, when gathered in religious ritual, are permitted to consume the hallucinogenic peyote cactus. The effects of the drug have been described as similar to those of mescaline, with feelings of a distortion of time, feelings of transcendence, mind and body separation, and tranquility. The court's decision in favor of the Native American Church was based primarily on the Church's relationship to the commonwealth and not on the social context of the group itself. For one thing, the Church's location in a remote part of the southwest isolated its members from the general population. For another, their use of the drug was not involved in the underground economy and thereby a threat to the market. Hence, the state could find no compelling reason that would forbid the use of peyote and thereby cause the state to interfere with the free exercise of religion. Their use of peyote was strictly spiritual and had no relationship to the development of an alternative economy (*People v. Woody* 1964).

Thus far, Rastafarian groups have not met with similar success. In the late 1970s, the state supreme court in Miami, Florida, enjoined the Coptic Church, an affiliate of the Rastafarian movement, from the use of marijuana. The rejection of the Church's proposal for the legal use of marijuana was based on its inability to demonstrate to the court that the behavior was not a threat to the common welfare. Indeed, the members of the Church were known for using vehicles on city streets while under the influence of the drug. The state's interest here was too pressing to allow an exemption from the drug laws. However, one justice did dissent from the majority opinion and held that the church could regulate its use of marijuana in much the same way that the Native American Church controlled its use of peyote.

More recent discussion has elaborated on the position of the dissenting justice in the Miami case and forcefully argued for an accommodation of the Rastas within a valid drug law. The reasoning in the argument identifies the Rastafarian movement as a mystical religion whose adherents believe that the use of marijuana is a divine ordinance. Supporters of this position cited a work on the Rastas that describes their use of marijuana as follows:

> [It] produces psycho-spiritual effects and has socio-religious functions especially for people under stress. It produces visions, heightens unity and communal feelings, dispels gloom and fear and brings tranquility to the mind of the dispossessed. (Barrett 1977)

This would lead us to believe that when the Rastas use ganja, their practice mirrors the religious rituals of the Native American Church. This interpretation of their use of marijuana, however, overlooks the sociopolitical interpretation that Rastas give to herb: the smoking of the chalice of marijuana is an experience that enlightens Rastas to the ever-present threat of slavery and degradation. Through its use they can find strength to live in "an entire nontraditional and alternate system of power and control, influence and prestige." The chalice of marijuana helps transform the Rasta into a rebel rather than a tranquil citizen, which is what peyote does among the members of the Native American Church. Fortified by ganja, for instance, Ras boldly identifies the social milieu of the dominant society around him a "this shitism called Babylon." Indeed, urban Rastas like Rabu, Rashi and Ras do not share the presuppositions and preoccupations found in the dominant society around them. Marijuana use among the Rastas empowers them to seize their own historical process. This makes accommodation with mainstream society difficult. This is a contrast to the peyote rituals, which help the Native American escape from degradation in mystical ways, which does not seem to present as strong a threat to the dominant cultural mode.

Rebellious Rastas

The cultural ways of rebellious Rastas relieve their emotions of anger and frustration which arise from their sense of victimization by the system. Their ethos also provides them with a means of escaping this oppression. For if one's body is the ultimate text upon which the power of the state and the economy is inscribed—what philosopher Michel Foucault has called "political anatomy"—the bodies of the Rastas do not bear that inscription. Since they are not docile to the discipline of the factory nor of the wage, their acquisition of wealth has little in common with the rules of the market economy, and they grow wealthy through their own means of cooperation.

Within the American legal system these Rastas appear intractable. As a less developed capitalist nation, Jamaica has not yet fully developed a formal legal system with the demands for rationality and universality that American jurisprudence has. Thus, we can expect that in contrast with the American legal system, Jamaican courts would be more willing to accommodate Rastas when they are brought to trial on issues that relate to their culture. Indeed, ever since independence, cases dealing with Rastas do seem less of a threat to the Jamaican rule of law, and there are indications of an *ad hoc* dispensation of justice rather than applications of statutory law to particular cases.

A study of twelve court cases in which Rastas were involved demonstrates that the American legal system has never seriously considered a form in which Rastas could freely exercise their cultural beliefs. Instead, the attitudinal bias which has been noted within the judiciary process is likely to affix the label of vegetarian sect or Jamaican cult to the Rasta. Where the possibility of religious exemption does arise for the Rastas, this is always discussed in terms that exclude their sale of marijuana and other nonreligious usages of the herb. In Jamaica the situation is somewhat different, especially since the granting of independence to the island nation in 1962.

In 1965, for instance, an appeal was heard in Kingston concerning a Rastafarian defendant which overturned an earlier decision by a resident magistrate in St. Catherine parish. There, a Rasta had been convicted of unlawful possession of money. The magistrate had decided the case on the basis of the testimony of the arresting officer who was familiar with the Rasta and asserted that the Rasta had no legal way to obtain such money in his possession. The Rasta responded that the money was "fe we brethren. Is I man money." Nevertheless, the magistrate in St. Catherine had convicted him. On appeal the conviction was quashed because, as the court pointed out, the money could have indeed been the property of some Rastas who put it in the custody of the defendant. The first magistrate had erred in convicting the Rasta defendant because there was no fact upon which reasonable suspicion could be entertained that the money was unlawfully obtained. Interestingly, no reference was made to the well-known fact that Rastas also obtained money through the sale of marijuana, a violation of the Dangerous Drugs Act of Jamaica.

In 1971 another court case demonstrated how willing the Jamaican judiciary was to recognize the Rastafarian movement as a subculture without referring to the issue of whether or not the Rastas were engaging in the sale of marijuana or involved in an alternate economy. The case involved Rastas who were charged with assault and damage of a bus. They were convicted, but one of the defendants, Hines, won an appeal because the judge at his trial did not allow him to "swear by Almighty God, King Rastafari." Hines explained his reasons to the judge for the new form of oath:

> I do not want to make any alteration or legislate any law in this European court or this court room. This is, as I referred to you before, according to the ancient council of the ancient dread, according to the order of Melchisedech which has neither beginning nor ending of days, who worship the true and living God that sits on the throne of David, and being at the very first instance refused to be accepted, I think I will not on any occasion proceed in taking any oath, for I explain why. (*Jamaica Law Reports* 1971)

The judge stated that the oath Hines wished to take was unlawful.

The appeals court overturned the judge's conviction of Hines. It said that the form in which Hines wished "to take the oath was considered with that professed belief . . . declared by him to be binding on his conscience and . . . he would have become subject to the provisions of the Perjury Law." Here we see that the Jamaican legal system is more open than other more formal systems of law to cultural, ethical and particularistic considerations.

In Jamaica, the ideals of the law as blind and universalistic can be put aside in favor of a system of law that accepts "local knowledge." General principles that can be applied to a wide range of different situations are avoided, and each case is judged on its own circumstances.

We have seen that the American legal system, based on an advanced capitalist market, contrasts markedly with that of Jamaica. The American court system is likely to deal with Rastas and their acquisition of large sums of money in less than benign ways. A 1982 federal case clearly demonstrates the presuppositions that are operative when the American system of jurisprudence has before it a Rasta convicted of illegal possession of money.

This case contrasts with the similar one in Jamaica mentioned above. In 1982, the federal government of the United States tried two Rastas caught trafficking in marijuana, but ascertained the fact only through an examination of the Rastas' beliefs, for they were not apprehended in the act of dealing itself. The Rasta had in their possession amounts of money which totaled about $87,000. They were arrested after the discovery of marijuana and the cash in their car during a routine check for a speeding violation. One admitted that he was a Rastafarian and involved in the sale of marijuana both for the consumption of the Rastas as well as for sale to rich Americans. He explained how the profits were used to support the group and help the poor in Jamaica. The American court, however, found his appeal to the Rastafarian culture irrelevant. It seized the money because it was the product of illegal activity and deported the Rastas because they were Jamaican immigrants.

Rastas may be declared outlaws because they resist the bourgeois imagination embedded in social behavior such as the accumulation of wealth for the sake of investment, the advancement of economic strategies for the development of the state, and an allegiance to a political and legal process that protects private property. The legal framework of statutory law cannot dialogue with these Rastas because the discourses are antithetical from the start, and the one cannot sustain the truth, virtues and values of the other. Thus, the social drama is played out between some Rastas and the larger community. The conflicts flow from the social life each type of discourse is intended to legitimize. American society prefers redress of grievances through labor unions, due process and universal rights that are applicable to all the citizenry regardless of any individual's particularity and cultural identity. This logic of the state and the law conflicts with the world of the unassimilated Rastas for whom cultural identity rests somewhere else than in the labor market, namely, a sense of black ethnicity rooted in Africa. What capitalist societies label as criminal behavior, then, the Rastas simply call justice. They are convinced that their behavior restores an equilibrium to living conditions after suffering the unemployment, racism and prejudice which Babylon has inflicted on them.

There is an obvious problem in all of this. How can the advanced capitalist state legitimize the justice that the Rastas have in place without thereby dissolving society into substantive particularities that war with each other for a privileged position? Accommodation for those Rastas who remain outside the legitimate marketplace of production and distribution seems to contradict the very foundations of capitalism and socialism. However, accommodation is more of a possibility when the adherents of Rastafari organize and present themselves as members of a religious group comparable to recognized religions. This action can only come about when those Rastas interested in accommodation remove the dynamics of Rastafari from the public domain of economics and rest them instead within the private domain of a citizen's conscience. The movement then will no longer be a means to produce, distribute and consume goods. With this transformation exemptions for Rastas will be easier because they "will remain limited to truly deserving Rastafarians while the state will maintain an effective deterrent against the commercial marijuana trade" (Taylor 1984).

12

Rastafari as a
Social Movement
Between Charisma and Institution

When the world depression threatened wage labor and capital accumulation in the early 1930s, an opportunity arose to rekindle the Jamaican peasantry, then a culture on the wane. Indeed, the depression acted as catalyst in the struggle between world capitalism and an indigenous, self-sufficient peasantry. This historical struggle merely peaked in the 1930s, for its roots reached far back. Ever since emancipation, the Jamaican peasantry had enjoyed a tradition rich in self-sufficient entrepreneurialism and a staunch independence from wage labor as the sole means of subsistence. In the midst of what was probably the final confrontation between capital and the peasantry in Jamaica, the Rastafarian movement emerged to champion the cause of the peasantry. Rather than clamoring for direct political or economic involvement in the power structures of the state, the movement burst forth with a symbolic consciousness that legitimated the traditional independence of the Jamaican peasantry. Absent from the vision of its founders was the development of capitalism, socialism and the spawning of a national state.

As a social movement, the Rasta brethren ignored the methods of reproduction through which bourgeois society was trying to ensure its survival and confirm its place in the Jamaican consciousness. Instead, the Rastas drew different boundaries for themselves. They disavowed the material reproduction of capitalist society by failing to engage in the labor movement to any appreciable degree.

They broke with the religious faith of the bourgeois world by rejecting the established Christian churches and the spiritualistic beliefs of the Jamaican poor. In their place they made a divinity of Haile Selassie and gave a sacred meaning to Ethiopia. Instead of political participation in Jamaican society, they called for repatriation to Ethiopia. They used ganja, a common practice in the thirties among the poor, but they transformed it into something other than an opiate to survive a toilsome day of labor in the fields. They found a meaning in its sensuous effects that freed them from enslavement to the wage and the subordinate role of worker.

In the early days of Rastafari, accounts of arrests, imprisonments and raids abounded. Charges of sedition, insanity, disturbing the peace, obscenity in public places, and the use of violence were all common complaints brought against this rowdy group of black men and women. At one point in 1960 some Rasta had even attempted to set up an armed guerilla camp in the hills around Kingston, but they were detected and executed.

In the early days of the movement, the Rastas withdrew from the dominant society, squatted on land they called their own, named their homesteads "Zion" and became self-sufficient. They resembled the declining peasantry because they believed so fully in their own jurisdiction over the land. They had emphatically little in common with the emerging bourgeoisie or even the despondent poor and unemployed who waited on the dole of the state and church. Yet, the Rastas were not revolutionary guards, for they had no economic program or progressive vision of the future of the Jamaican state. Perhaps the primary impact of the movement was symbolic: they overturned the image of the black man as a happy-go-lucky "quashie" and refused to accept the place that the Jamaican mulattos and white elites had reserved for the blacks.

As suggested in chapter 1, explanations for the dynamics of the Rasta movement have ranged from a revolutionary analysis to a mystical one. Those who view Rastafari from a revolutionary perspective suggest that its central thrust has been the betterment of the living conditions of the poor, a more equitable distribution of wealth, and the like. The writings of Horace Campbell, for instance, interpret the movement as a rational scheme based on practical reasoning which aims at resisting capitalist expansion and commodification. Campbell perceived in the Rastafarian movement a systemic program that directly confronted private ownership of the means of production. The apex of the revolutionary aspect of the movement arrived, he thought, when over four hundred Rastas joined the People's Liberation Army of Grenada which helped overthrow the administration of Eric Gairy in 1979.

Other analysts such as George Simpson and Shelia Kitzinger, however, focusing on the nonrational components of the movement, define Rastas essentially as mystics and rebels. Yet even their studies indicate that the movement had a socio-economic component. It interfered with the production of psychic and social deportments necessary for a person to function in capitalist society. The Rastas turned from the institutions and statuses that were legitimating the modernization of Jamaica in the 1930s and continue to persist in a cultural enclosure that shields them from participating in the capitalist discipline of the labor force.

The theoretical perspectives mentioned are determined by a rational and formal analysis that depends heavily on economic factors. Among the theorists who have not been so heavily influenced by an economic perspective are Joseph Owens (1976) and John Homiak (1985). They neither explain the Rastas as escapists nor do they rationalize the Rastas' religious beliefs. Instead, their participation in the lives of Rastas in Kingston moved them to focus on the creative role that religion could play in a stratified society. In Owens's view, just as the religion of the oppressor had been an important ideological weapon in the subjugation of a people, so too could the oppressed resist that hegemony through a religion of liberation. The Rastafari movement was just such a religion. Homiak drew attention to the oral tradition in the culture of Rastafari. This opened up the community of Rastafari to ongoing development through mutual dialogue. Discussing their creation of a sacred history, he wrote: "Theirs is a distinctive tradition in which the word is central to a collective quest for meaning and inspiration . . . and to the celebration of community and identity."

Most students have observed Rastafari from a single moment in time, and have ignored the changing social contexts in which the movement actually exists. In the United States, for example, a long-range viewpoint over several decades allows us to understand the transformation of the movement, which began as a resistance to the reproduction of a bourgeois lifestyle but became, in part, a lifestyle that the dominant society could accommodate. In Jamaica, on the other hand, a less developed country where the political, legal, and religious systems of society are still seeking to legitimize an expanding capitalist economy and preserve law and order, we have a different situation. There the movement has been transformed into a rational and religious option, a viable cultural alternative to bourgeois society, which, nevertheless, can co-opt the Rastafari when they threaten to disturb its equilibrium.

It is my argument that the Rastas developed as but one response

Conventional religious and social concepts are rejected by Rastas, who have fashioned their own beliefs about status and divinity. (Richard Kenefick)

to the need for spontaneous community and anti-structure that must flow through society from time to time. I believe that the Rastas truly launched their movement because of their "desire for freedom, liberation and self-determination." In Rastafari, statuses are temporarily suspended and roles are obstructed. Like the trickster in ancient mythology and folklore, the Rasta movement rendered possible an experience of what was forbidden. The image of the trickster which emerges in demonic form has its destructive tendencies, but ultimately it is a healing source for society. Yet these potentially beneficial tendencies in Rastafari, its demonic and trickster forces, are seldom given priority in the analysis of the movement, perhaps because that would not suit the purposes of the law enforcement agencies or other organs of highly developed capitalist nations that have to deal with it.

An American police officer once made the following remarks about a group of Rastas that he considered to be authentic representatives of the movement: "These are the Rastas who observe and respect our laws and procedures. They don't get into trouble. They are peace lovers. These Rastas don't get involved in the drug trade. They don't use brutal violence on each other, and they don't carry weapons concealed under their tams." The officer held firm to his belief that the Rastas who collide with American law are not true Rastas but outlaws that are hiding behind the religious guise of the Rastafarian movement.

This positive attitude toward the Rastafarian religion is not new, and for some time students of American jurisprudence have been arguing for legal accommodations on behalf of the religious beliefs of Rastas. In *Barnes vs. Government of the Virgin Islands* prison authorities were ordered to take reasonable steps to provide Rastas with diets in accord with their religious beliefs. In a case in the state of Michigan, where a prosecuting attorney suggested that the Rastas were a cultic group intending to wipe out the police force, this assertion was deemed an unwarranted attitudinal bias sufficient to have the Rasta defendant's conviction for assault with intent to commit murder overturned. Recently in New York State, attorneys have won rights for Rasta prisoners to wear their hair in their natural dreads.

On the other hand, the appeal by the Ethiopian Coptic Church to legalize the use of marijuana for religious purposes was not successful and accommodation for religious practices has only been granted in those instances where this has not compromised the goals of the secular law. In general, however, the arguments have been mounting in the literature of American jurisprudence to accommodate the "Soul Rebels," as the Rastas are called in the music of Bob Marley. These arguments for accommodation are only partial, for they do not include accommodation of the underground economy that Rastas deploy, but rather categorize the movement only as a religion understood in a Eurocentric way.

In Jamaica, where a weak market economy has not generated the legal rationality characteristic of the United States, there is a broader understanding of Rastafari. There, local knowledge still persists and the influence of local groups is strong. Thus, as we have

Reggae musician Bob Marley called the Rastas "Soul Rebels." (AP/Wide World Photos)

seen, Rasta symbolism, language and beliefs flowered in the Jamaican election of the 1970s.

The I-n-I language of the brethren, their allusions to exile in Babylon and their many slogans were freely used by the People's National Party under the chairmanship of Michael Manley. Throughout his electoral campaign, Manley used Rastafarian symbolism to attract the black consciousness of Jamaica and align it with his socialist policy of economic reorganization. By 1976 both the Jamaican Labour Party and the People's National Party were using Rastafarian symbolism. The *Daily Gleaner*, the nation's bourgeois newspaper, was also reporting Rastafarian events such as the journey some Rastas made to Ethiopia.

Throughout the 1980s the Rastas have participated in Jamaican national events through their performances as artists, musicians and spokespersons for the patriotic spirit of Jamaica. They have operated shops in Kingston which range from reggae music outlets to ital food restaurants. Even the police, the enemy of the Rastas under colonial rule, now recognize that they are part of the Jamaican culture. While many Rastas live in fishing villages or hustle for their livelihood, some do live in the middle-class housing developments sponsored by the government. While some Rastas still defiantly oppose the Urban Development Corporation and refuse to move from their homesteads carved out of beachfront lands, others talk about Haile Selassie and Babylon on the verandas of their comfortable homes overlooking Kingston harbor.

Social scientists have argued that advanced capitalist societies cannot tolerate spontaneous expressions of community, such as the Rastas manifest. But Jamaican society, located betwixt and between an advanced market economy and one based on local entrepreneurial activity and patronage, has a greater tolerance for spontaneous community. Hence, while the Rastas' dealings in marijuana, their mocking of authority, their resistance to birth control, their frequent refusal to send their children to school, and their subordination of women to the men fly in the face of bourgeois liberal ideas, they are not subject to forceful reprisal from above. The Rastas flourish in Jamaica because the working-class ethic and capitalist dynamic are still subordinate to cultural particularities. In independent Jamaica, with its less developed markets and economic decline, the Rastas have found a cultural niche that goes beyond mere religious toleration. I believe that the Jamaican legal system winks at their alternate entrepreneurial activities because Jamaicans themselves do not depend entirely on the free market for their sustenance, certainly not to the degree that the United States does.

In the United States, bourgeois culture has demonstrated its hegemony by absorbing alternate lifestyles, learning how to use them to serve its own profitable pursuits. Through its attachments to the music and entertainment industries, aspects of Rastafarian culture have become capitalized and commodified. The growth of the industries around reggae and Rastafarian symbols are witnesses to this.

Many theorists call for the Rastafari movement to accommodate itself to the needs of the modern world. One West Indian scholar, a Rasta himself, commented that the movement is bound to fail as just another ideological dream if it cannot articulate a persuasive plan for the renovation and revitalization of society. To be sure, some adherents of Rastafari have transformed it into a rational institution by turning it toward the dynamics of a religious, aesthetic or political movement. Rastas attend universities, become lawyers, writers and even revolutionaries. All of these are nuances of the Rastafarian movement that lean toward a practical rationality. Here the goals and tenets of Rastafari point toward economic productivity, better access to resources, and the strengthening of a state based on universal justice. But a price is paid: the spontaneity that was expressed in the midst of the Jamaican society during the turmoil of the 1930s is on the wane.

Those who enjoy spontaneity are Rastas like Rabu, Rahi and Baba. They survive through their own communal economies, live by hustling and look to Africa as their true homeland. These are the Rastas who can deal in the herb on a heavy scale and consume money in partying, buying expensive clothes and cars or just lending it out to friends. These Rastas have many wives, many children and believe in their own invincibility—even in the face of the law—because Jah will protect them. They believe that they will prevail in the long run, and this even while the police raid their smoke shops. And, when jailed on charges of dealing in drugs, they express no fear of the system.

The origin of Rastafari as a disquieting social movement is expressed at the crisis points in capitalist society. Here the tenets of Rastafari are the optional ways for redressing grievances in society by those who have not been seduced by the symbolic world of capitalism. Wherever the hold of bourgeois culture is tenuous and people reason through other ways to understand the inequality of riches and stratification, there the images of Rastafari are bound to emerge as one possible response, especially for a black man or woman. Such Rastas are not simply aesthetic performers. They are social dramatists who collide with the police officers and the organized church. More than this, however, they connect with a waning tradition of chicanery in the West, its ribaldry and rowdiness, its debauchery and fervor, certainly evident in preindustrialized societies, and ever diminishing in less developed countries as the rationalization of economic structures increases. With economic centralization by state or corporation, we can expect to witness the

Rastafari movement turning from its spontaneous origins and generating legitimate performers, writers and business professionals. Perhaps the success of reggae music epitomizes the institutionalization of the movement into the rational programs of modern society. This might cause us to forget that the dynamic of Rastafari originally lay not in an aesthetic, religious or political platform but in the preservation of the peasant world and a prebourgeois society. I believe that Rastas who defy our bourgeois sense of law and order remind us that the symbols of Rastafari celebrate the spontaneity of a community whose social roots were in the Jamaican peasantry.

So where are the Rastas today? The brethren and sisters in the modern world roam between the fervor of charisma and the quiescence of institutionalization. Will they become the leaders of the black community in the years ahead? The rebels with a blueprint for a new society? I don't know.

Cited References and Selected Bibliography

Barrett, Leonard. *The Rastafarians*. Boston: Beacon Press, 1977.

Bishton, Derek. *Black Heart Man: A Journey into Rasta*. London: Chatton & Windus, 1986.

Campbell, Horace. "Rastafari: Culture of Resistance." *Race and Class*, xxii, 1 , pp. 1–22, 1980.

_____. *Rasta and Resistance*. Trenton: African World Press, 1987.

Chevannes, Barry. *Social Origins of the Rastafari Movement*. Kingston: Institute of Social and Economic Research, University of West Indies, 1978.

Geertz, Clifford. *Local Knowledge*. New York: Basic Books, 1983.

Homiak, John P. *The "Ancient of Days" Seated Black: Eldership, Oral Tradition, 2nd Ritual in Rastafari Culture*. Ann Arbor: University Microfilm, 1985.

Kitzinger, Shelia. "The Rastafari Brethren in Jamaica." *Comparative Studies in Society and History*, ix, pp. 30–41, 1966.

Lewis, William. "The Rastafari: Millennial Cultists or Unregenerate Peasants?" *Peasant Studies*, vol. 14, no. 1 (Fall), pp. 5–26, 1986.

Owens, Joseph. *Dread*. Kingston: Sangster, 1976.

Posner, Richard. "An Economic Theory of the Criminal Law." *Columbia Law Review*, vol. 85/86, pp. 1193–1231, 1985.

Rodney, Walter. *The Groundings With My Brothers*. London: Villiers Publications, 1983.

Simpson, George. "The Ras-Tafari Movement in Jamaica: A Study of Race and Class Conflict." *Social Force*, vol. 34, no. 2, pp. 167–171, 1955.

Smith, M.G., Ray Augier, and Rex Nettleford. *The Ras-Tafari Movement in Kingston, Jamaica*. Kingston: Institute of Social and Economic Research, University College of the West Indies, 1960.

Steinberg, Stephen. *The Ethnic Myth*. Boston: Beacon Press, 1981.

Taylor, Timothy. "Soul Rebels: The Rastafarians and the Free Exercise Clause." *Georgetown Law Review*, vol. 72, (June), pp. 1605–1635, 1984.

Turner, Victor. *The Ritual Process*. Chicago: Aldine, 1969.

Watson, Llewellyn. "Social Structures and Social Movements: The Black Muslims in the U.S.A. and the Rastafarians in Jamaica." *British Journal of Sociology*, xxiv, no. 2 (June), pp. 188–198, 1973.

William F. Lewis *received his Ph.D. in Anthropology from the New School for Social Research, and had, in addition, graduate degrees in Music, Theology, and Philosophy. His work on the Rastafarian movement and on cultural and legal pluralism was presented in papers at many anthropological meetings and in scholarly journals; he was a Mellon Seminar participant in 1990. Lewis was a member of the Society for Humanistic Anthropology, and as a Franciscan Brother, he strove to bring the perspectives of humanist cultural anthropology to his church community.*

Serena Nanda *is Professor and Chair of the Department of Anthropology at John Jay College (City University of New York). She is the author of* Cultural Anthropology *(Wadsworth), currently in its fifth edition, and* Neither Man Nor Woman: The Hijras of India *(Wadsworth, 1990), an ethnography of a religious cult and community of ritual performers who occupy a third sex and gender role in India. Her current research is on cultural diversity and law in the United States; she is co-author of* American Cultural Pluralism and Law *(Praeger, 1988).*

Joan Young Gregg *is Professor in College English as a Second Language at New York City Technical College (City University of New York) and the author of several textbooks in college composition. She has received two PSC-CUNY Research Foundation Awards for research in medieval religious narrative and is a 1993 recipient of an NEH Summer Seminar grant for study of the Jew in medieval literature.*